There Are Tittles in This Title

By the same author:
NUMBERLAND

There Are Tittles in This Title

The Weird World of Words

The Weird World of Words

Mitchell Symons

Michael O'Mara Books Limited

First published in Great Britain in 2014 by

Michael O'Mara Books Limited
9 Lion Yard
Tremadoc Road
London SW4 7NQ

A CIP catalogue record for this book is available from the British Library.

Papers used by Michael O'Mara Books Limited are natural, recyclable products made from wood grown in sustainable forests. The manufacturing processes conform to the environmental regulations of the country of origin.

ISBN: 978-1-78243-257-9 in hardback print format

ISBN: 978-1-78243-271-5 in e-book format

1 2 3 4 5 6 7 8 9 10

Cover design by Claire Cater
Illustrations by Andrew Pinder

Designed and typeset by K. DESIGN, Winscombe, Somerset

Printed and bound by CPI Group (UK) Ltd, Croydon, CR0 4YY

www.mombooks.com

To Penny

With love and thanks for
thirty wonderful years

Contents

Contents

Introduction

I had so much fun compiling *Numberland*, a book devoted to number-related trivia, that I decided to do the same for words. I wanted to call it *Wordworld*, (a bit of) a pun on *Numberland*, but my publisher, Louise Dixon, suggested *There Are Tittles in This Title*. Once she explained to me what a tittle was (a dot above the 'i'), I was all for it. The truth is, even after some sixty-odd books (the books weren't odd – well, not ALL of them – but the figure is approximate and therefore 'odd'), I'm useless at titles – except for other people's books where I'm surprisingly inventive. Just can't do it for myself.

So much for the title. The book itself was pure joy to compile. Among the many things I learned, my absolute favourite was an obsolete English word – scurryfunge – which means a hasty tidying of the house between the time you see a neighbour and the time she knocks on the door. What's not to like? I hope you have as much fun reading this as I did writing it.

Now for some acknowledgements:

I'd like to thank my wonderful publisher Louise Dixon, with whom I've worked for some twenty years without ever having a cross word (which must be some kind of record). My editor, Gabriella Nemeth, has done a fine job of turning the sow's ear I sent her into the silk purse you have before you. My thanks also to Emily Banyard for her amazing PR work. A big word of praise too for the illustrator, Andrew Pinder, and the designers, Claire Cater and Kay Hayden.

In addition, I'd also like to thank the following people for their help, contributions and/or support: Gilly Adams, Jenny Garrison, Nicholas Ridge, Charlie Symons, Jack Symons, Louise Symons, Penny Symons, David Thomas, Martin Townsend, Clair Woodward and Rob Woolley.

Mitchell Symons

2014

The Names of Things You Didn't Know Had Names

Adelaster: meaning 'unknown star' in Greek, this is the name given to newly discovered plants awaiting classification by botanists

Aglet: the plastic covering on the end of a shoelace

Aphthongs: silent letters in words such as 'know' and 'psychology'

Armsate: the hole in a shirt or a jumper through which you put your hand and arm

Bonnet: the cap on a fire hydrant

Brannock device: the metal instrument used in shoe shops to measure feet

Brassard: a band worn around the arm

Buccula: a person's double chin

Chanking: food that's spat out

Columella: the bottom part of the nose that separates the nostrils

Contrail: the thin line of cloud that forms behind an aircraft at high altitudes

Diastema: a gap between the front teeth

Drupelets: the bumps on raspberries

Epithalamium: a poem written to celebrate a wedding

Eyes: the holes in Swiss cheese

Ferrule: the metal band on the top of a pencil that holds the eraser in place

F-hole: the S-shaped opening in a violin

Fillip: the technical term for snapping your fingers

Gambrinous: the state of being full of beer

Griffonage: illegible handwriting

Gruntle: a pig's snout

Harp: the metal hoop a lampshade sits on

IDEO locator: the 'you are here' arrow on a map

Jiffy: 1/100th of a second

Keeper: the loop on a belt that holds the end in place after it has passed through the buckle

Lalochezia: the use of swearing to relieve stress or pain

Lemniscate: the infinity symbol

Lunt: a puff of smoke, such as that produced when someone smokes a pipe

Lunula: the white tip of the finger and toenail (because the end of the nail is rounded like the moon)

Minimus: the little finger or toe

Mucophagy: the consumption of the nasal mucus obtained from nose-picking

Nemophilia: the love of spending time in forests.

Nittles: the punctuation marks designed to denote swear words in comics

Obdormition: when an arm or a leg goes to 'sleep' as a result of numbness caused by pressure on a nerve

Octothorpe: the 'pound' key (#)

Ophyron: the space between your eyebrows

Pandiculation: the act of stretching and yawning

Peen: on a hammer, the end opposite the striking face

Pips: the little bumps on the surface of a table tennis bat

Porcelator: the little hole in the sink that lets water drain out instead of flowing over the side

Purlicue: the space between the extended thumb and index finger

Rasceta: the creases on the inside of your wrist

Rowel: the revolving star on the back of a cowboy's spurs

Saddle: the rounded part on the top of a book of matches

Sillage: the faint trace of perfume left in the wake of a passing person

Snarge: the remains of birds hit by aeroplanes in flight

Tines: the prongs on forks

Tittle: the dot above the letter 'i'

Toque: a chef's tall hat

Tragus: the little lump of flesh just in front of the ear canal

Truck: the ball on top of a flagpole

Ullage: the word for empty space between the bottle top and the liquid

Vamp: the upper front part of a shoe

Vibrissae: a cat's whiskers

Walla: a sound engineer's term for room noise

Zarf: a holder for a cup or a mug without handles

There is no single word for the back of the knee

A Word to the Wise 1

Did you know...

Stewardesses is the longest word that is typed with only the left hand.

✳

The only fifteen-letter word that can be spelled without repeating a letter is **uncopyrightable.**

✳

Hull City is the only British league football team that hasn't got any letters you can fill in with a pencil.

✳

If you mouth the word **colourful** to someone, it looks like you are saying, **I love you.**

✳

Knightsbridge is the place with the most consonants in a row.

✳

Just **1,000** words make up ninety per cent of all writing.

✳

No word in the English language rhymes with **orange, silver** or **month.**

Dreamt is the only English word that ends in the letters **mt**

✳

Queue is the only word in the English language
to be pronounced the same way even if the last four
letters are removed.

✳

**Zenith, tariff, sherbet, algebra, carafe, syrup, cotton,
mattress** and **alcohol** are all derived from Arabic.

✳

Almost is the longest word in the English language with all
the letters in alphabetical order.

✳

Appeases, arraigning, hotshots, signings and
teammate all have letters which occur twice and
only twice.

✳

The syllable **-ough** can be pronounced nine different
ways – as evidenced by the following sentence: 'A rough,
dough-faced, thoughtful ploughman emerged from a
slough to walk through the streets of Scarborough,
coughing and hiccoughing.'

✳

The sentence **He believed Caesar could see people
seizing the seas** contains seven different spellings of
the 'ee' sound.

Fun with Words

Words that are rarely used in the singular:

trivia (singular: trivium)   minutiae (minutia)
paparazzi (paparazzo)   grafitti (grafitto)
assizes (assize)   scampi (scampo)
auspices (auspice)   scruples (scruple)
timpani (timpano)   measles (measle)

Words that are rarely used in the positive:

(in)advertent   (in)corrigible
(im)maculate   (im)placable
(in)clement   (in)effable
(dis)consolate   (un)wieldy
(in)delible   (in)nocuous,
(un)furl   (im)pervious
(in)sipid   (un)expurgated
(un)speakable   (im)peccable
(un)kempt   (in)evitable

WHERE'S IT FROM?

SNIPER

This goes back to the days when marksmen would hone their skills by shooting snipe (wading birds), hence the term 'sniper'.

Kangaroo Words

A kangaroo word is one which contains the letters – in the correct order – of a synonym. For example, the word 'masculine' contains the words 'male' and 'man'.

acc**ust**om**ed**
ac**r**id
ad**roit**ness
aff**ect**
ag**grava**t**ed**
allocate
al**one**
amic**able**
app**lauded**
apposite
appropriate
a**stound**
barricade
bec**ause**
b**efore**
bloss**om**

bombard
burst
calumn**ies**
capsule
cartoon
cata**comb**
charis**ma**
chick**en**
chocola**te**
cloistered
cont**ami**nate
curtail
damsel
dece**ased**
de**ception**
deli**be**r**ated**

de**mean**ing
departed
dep**artm**ent
depository
des**truction**
di**minutive**
dis**appointed**
hostelry
enc**our**age
ent**wined**
exha**usted**
ex**ists**
factual
falsi**fied**

WHERE'S IT FROM?

MONEY CALLED 'BREAD'

It comes from Cockney rhyming slang: 'Give me your money. Give me your bread and honey'.

Anti-Kangaroo Words

By contrast, an anti-kangaroo word is one which contains the letters – in the correct order – of an antonym.

animos**ity**   **fa**bri**cation**   **r**ev**olution**
beard**ed**   **feasted**   **there**
com**mu**nicative   **friend**   tho**roughly**
court**eous**   **pest**   **unru**ffian**ly**
co**vert**   p**rud**ent   **wonderful**
effec**tive**   p**rurie**nt
exacer**bate**   **re**s**igned**

WHERE'S IT FROM?

HOOLIGANS

This is all down to a nineteenth century Irishman named Patrick Hooligan who was notorious for fighting – especially in bars. He was also incredibly strong, so much so that his party piece was to lift four large men on to his back and then stagger across the bar-room floor. After a while, his reputation for fighting spread so far that bars – even bars he had never visited – would put up signs saying that Hooligan wouldn't be served. Eventually, his name became an eponym – that is to say that any brawling man would be called a hooligan.

Words That Changed Their Meaning Over Time

Awful

Original meaning: 'inspiring wonder'. Short version of 'full of awe'

❖

Bimbo

Original meaning: from *bambino* – the Italian word for 'little child', it once meant 'fellow' or 'one of the boys'

❖

Bully

Original meaning: 'darling' or 'sweetheart'

❖

Nice

Original meaning: 'foolish' or 'silly'

❖

Chocolate

Original meaning: from *choc-atl* – an Aztec word that meant 'bitter water'

❖

Amazed

Original meaning: 'alarmed' or 'terrified'

Artificial

Original meaning: 'full of artistic skill'

◆

Stultify

Original meaning: 'to declare insane'

◆

Girl

Original meaning: 'a young person of either sex'

◆

Basement

Original meaning: 'toilet'

WHERE'S IT FROM?

GOBBLEDYGOOK

It's not often that you can pinpoint the first time a word or phrase was used but this is an exception. On 30 March 1944, a man named Maury Maverick, a Congressman who was serving as the chairman of the United States Smaller War Plants Corporation, wrote a memo to staff banning what he called 'gobbledygook language'. He went on to write that 'anyone using the words *activation* or *implementation* will be shot'. Later, when the word began to be used by other people, Maverick explained that the word was based on the turkey which was 'always gobbledy gobbling and strutting with ludicrous pomposity. At the end of his gobble, there was a sort of gook.'

Obsolete Words That Are Ripe for a Comeback

Bezonter
Expletive expressing surprise or consternation

Bouffage
A satisfying meal

Cockalorum
Someone who has a high opinion of himself despite being very short

Condiddle
To make away (with something) secretly

Curglaff
The shock felt when one first plunges into cold water

Flippercanorious
Elegant

Illecebrous
Alluring, enticing, attractive

Irrisory
Addicted to laughing or sneezing

Lunting
Walking and smoking a pipe

Purfled
Short-winded, especially in consequence of being too lusty

Scurryfunge
A hasty tidying of the house between the time you see a neighbour and the time she knocks on the door

Snudge
To stride around as though you're terribly busy, when in fact you're doing absolutely nothing

Squizzle
To fire a gun

Wagpastie
A rogue

Portmanteau Words

These are words formed by combining two other words. Here are some that have passed into the English language:

advertorial, from advertising and editorial
bankster, from banker and gangster
biopic, from biographical and motion picture
blog, from web and log
Bollywood, from Bombay and Hollywood
chuggers, from charity and muggers
cyborg, from cybernetic and organism
endorphin, from endogenous and morphine
Frappuccino, from frappé and cappuccino
gaydar, from gay and radar
malware, from malicious and software
metrosexual, from metropolitan and heterosexual
mockney, from mock and Cockney
mocktail, from mock and cocktail
moobs, from man and boobs
netiquette, from (Inter)net and etiquette (similarly, **wikiquette**)
pixel, from picture and element
sexting, from sex and texting
skyjack, from sky and hijack

skype, from Sky and peer-to-peer

spork, from spoon and fork

staycation, from stay and vacation

Texmex, food from Texas and Mexico – i.e. Americanized Mexican food

Wikipedia, from wiki and encyclopedia

WHERE'S IT FROM?

IDIOT

The word 'idiot' originally comes from the Greek word *idiotes* which was used to refer to a person who was a private individual – or more specifically, one who was so preoccupied with their own personal life that they wouldn't take part in the democratic process.

In Latin, the word *idiota* came to mean 'uneducated or ignorant person' and it passed through to English – as so many words did – through the French. And that would have been that but for something extraordinary. Scientists decided to use the word idiot to classify mentally retarded people. Specifically, it meant that someone had a mental age of less than three years old and an intelligence quotient (IQ) under twenty-five.

Similarly, the word 'moron' – a word that, like idiot, is one we would only ever now use as an insult – was originally used to refer to an adult with a mental age of between eight and twelve.

Words Invented by William Shakespeare

The *Oxford English Dictionary* has verified that Shakespeare originated the following words or, at the very least, was the first to use them in print.

Admirable, Aerial, Amazement, Arch-villain, Arouse, Auspicious

❖

Barefaced, Bedazzle, Besmirch, Birthplace, Bloodstained, Bloodsucking

❖

Castigate, Clutch, Cold-blooded, Colourful, Comply, Countless, Critical

❖

Denote, Disgraceful, Dishearten, Distrustful, Domineering, Downstairs

❖

Educate, Employer, Engagement, Enmesh, Eventful, Exposure

❖

Fairyland, Fashionable, Fortune-teller, Foul-mouthed, Freezing, Frugal

Generous, Go-between, Grime, Grovel

❖

Hostile, Hot-blooded, Hurry

❖

Ill-tempered, Impartial, Impede, Invitation, Invulnerable

❖

Lament, Lapse, Laughable, Leapfrog, Lonely,
Love letter, Lustrous

❖

Majestic, Manager, Marketable, Misquote,
Monumental, Motionless

❖

Negotiate, Never-ending

❖

Obscene, Ode, Operate, Overrate

❖

Pageantry, Pander, Paternal, Perplex, Petition, Pious, Puke

❖

Quarrelsome

❖

Rant, Reclusive, Reinforcement, Reliance, Remorseless,
Restoration, Retirement

Sanctimonious, Savage, Scuffle, Shipwrecked,
Shooting star, Silliness, Soft-hearted, Squabble,
Stealthy, Successful, Swagger

◆

Tardiness, Torture, Tranquil

◆

Uncomfortable, Uneducated, Unhelpful, Unwillingness

◆

Vulnerable

◆

Well behaved, Well bred, Well educated, Well read

◆

Zany

NEWSPAPER HEADLINES

30 Year Friendship Ends At Altar

ALCOHOL ADS PROMOTE DRINKING

LARGER KANGAROOS LEAP
FARTHER, RESEARCHERS FIND

Phrases First Invented or Popularized by William Shakespeare

'A fool's paradise' (*Romeo and Juliet*)

★

'A tower of strength' (*Richard III*)

★

'Breathe one's last' (*Henry VI, Part 3*)

★

'Come full circle' (*King Lear*)

★

'Dead as a doornail' (*Henry VI, Part 2*)

★

'Eaten me out of house and home' (*Henry IV, Part 2*)

★

'Elbow room' (*King John*)

★

'Give the devil his due' (*Henry IV, Part 1*)

★

'Hoist with his own petard' (*Hamlet*)

'Let slip the dogs of war' (*Julius Caesar*)

★

'Love is blind' (*The Merchant of Venice*)

★

'Milk of human kindness' (*Macbeth*)

★

'My own flesh and blood' (*The Merchant of Venice*)

★

'Neither a borrower nor a lender be' (*Hamlet*)

★

'Once more unto the breach' (*Henry V*)

★

'One fell swoop' (*Macbeth*)

'Murder most foul' (*Hamlet*)

'Play fast and loose' (*Love's Labour's Lost*)

★

'Something in the wind' (*The Comedy of Errors*)

★

'Stood on ceremonies' (*Julius Caesar*)

★

'Strange bedfellows' (*The Tempest*)

'The be-all and the end-all' (*Macbeth*)

'The course of true love never did run smooth'
(*A Midsummer Night's Dream*)

'The naked truth' (*Love's Labour's Lost*)

★

'The world's mine oyster' (*The Merry Wives of Windsor*)

★

''Tis neither here nor there' (*Othello*)

★

'To make a virtue of necessity'
(*The Two Gentlemen of Verona*)

★

'Too much of a good thing' (*As You Like It*)

★

'We are such stuff as dreams are made on' (*The Tempest*)

★

'Wear my heart on my sleeve' (*Othello*)

★

'What the dickens' (*The Merry Wives of Windsor*)

★

'What's in a name?' (*Romeo and Juliet*)

The Origins of Expressions 1

SMART ALEC

Alex Hoag was a thief in the 1840s. He worked with his wife Miranda who was a prostitute. Alex would slip into the room where Miranda was working and steal her client's possessions. Alex would then return, posing as an angry jealous husband. The client would rush off, not caring that he'd been robbed. A smart Alex – or, as it became, Alec – indeed.

––––––

RED LETTER DAYS

This goes back to the early church almanacs when religious festivals and saints' days would be specially printed in red ink. Modern diaries and calendars maintained this tradition of distinguishing special days with the colour red and so nowadays any significant day – even if it's only significant to an individual (like their birthday) – is described as a red letter day.

––––––

THE WRONG SIDE OF THE BED

Historically, anything to do with the left-hand side was considered sinister (hence the Latin word *sinister* for 'left'). Innkeepers were not immune to this superstition and so would always ensure that the left side of the bed was pushed against a wall, so guests had no other option but to get up on the right (i.e. not the wrong) side of the bed.

THE CURSE OF SCOTLAND

Since the early eighteenth century, the nine of diamonds has been known as the Curse of Scotland. One suggestion for the reason is that every ninth king of Scotland is a tyrant; another that it was the winning card in a card game called comette, to which many Scots were addicted; others point to the story that the Duke of Cumberland, the Bloody Butcher, wrote his order to kill hostages on the card after the Battle of Culloden in 1746.

JUMPING THE SHARK

This refers to the moment when a TV show has run out of new ideas and resorts to absurd storylines. The expression comes from a crazy 1977 episode of *Happy Days*, where the Fonz did a waterski jump over a penned-in shark.

TIE THE KNOT

There are several possibilities. The Carthaginians used to tie the thumbs of the bride and bridegroom with a leather lace; in Ancient Rome, brides wore girdles that were tied in knots, which the groom had the job of untying; while in the Hindu marriage ceremony, the groom is required to tie a ribbon around the bride's neck.

BY HOOK OR BY CROOK

This one goes all the way back to medieval times when people – desperate for wood to use as fuel – were allowed to take branches and twigs that had fallen from trees on land owned by the Crown. These people weren't stupid and so, if they were farmers and had reapers (which looked like hooks) or if they were shepherds and had crooks, they'd do their utmost to get as much wood as possible by all the means at their disposal – or, in other words, by hook or by crook.

––––––

SPITTING IMAGE

Like so many phrases that have worked their way into our language, this is a result of a mispronunciation of a perfectly intelligible phrase. In the southern states of the United States, it used to be said of a boy who behaved and looked like his father that he was the 'spirit and image' of his father. From there, it's not hard to see how 'spirit and image' could evolve into 'spitting image'.

––––––

THE BRUSH OFF

In times gone by, hotel porters would look after guests by making sure that they looked immaculate just before they set out for the evening. The way they did this was to run a brush over a gentleman's clothing. Gentlemen who were known to tip badly didn't get much of a brushing down: instead, they got just a few strokes of the brush or in other words (and here we come to the origin of the expression) the 'brush off'.

IT'S NOT OVER TILL THE FAT LADY SINGS

The actual expression is 'the opera ain't over till the fat lady sings' and it was first used by a sportswriter named Dan Cook in 1976 – or thereabouts – in the *San Antonio Express-News* to indicate that the sporting contest wasn't over until time had been called. In employing such a colourful metaphor, he was assuming that in every opera, a soprano – usually amply proportioned – will sing an aria at the end. The popularity of this expression spread when, a couple of years later, Cook used it in broadcasts as a commentator. He was trying to console local basketball fans who were dejected because the San Antonio Spurs were down three games to one in the play-offs against the Washington Bullets. The Washington Bullets coach, Dick Motta, heard the broadcast and used the expression himself to caution fans against overconfidence then and in subsequent matches, and the phrase became the team's rallying cry. From there, it entered the English language – albeit erroneously.

THE COLD SHOULDER

This has its roots in something quite specific. In olden times, when an unwanted visitor came you gave them cold shoulder of mutton instead of hot meat as a hint that they shouldn't call again.

SPRING CHICKEN

In the US, chicken farmers sold most of their chickens in the spring and so birds born at that time (or just before) were more valuable than the older birds that had survived the winter. Some farmers tried to sell the old birds at the same price as the younger ones. Buyers with a shrewd eye would know not to buy a bird that was 'no spring chicken' and so the term came to represent anything or anyone past their prime.

RED HERRING

A red herring is an irrelevance – something that distracts attention from important things.

In the nineteenth century, a red herring was another name for the smoked herring or kipper. During a hunt, if someone wanted to distract the hounds from following the scent of an animal, then they would put down a kipper (or red herring) and this would work extremely well. In fact, huntsmen themselves, when training their hounds, would use red herrings so that their dogs would learn to ignore the stronger smell and continue to follow the weaker scent of a fox or a badger. From there, it isn't hard to see why the expression was used to describe the laying of false clues in detective novels.

———

THE CAT GOT YOUR TONGUE?

There are two possibilities. The first is that it refers to the cat-o'-nine-tails – the whip used by the English Navy for flogging which caused so much pain that its victims were left speechless. The second possibility is that it refers to the practice of cutting out the tongues of liars and blasphemers and feeding them to animals (including cats).

———

BURY THE HATCHET

This goes back to the days when Native American tribes fought with one another. Eventually, when one side had had enough, they would throw a tomahawk into the ground and the other side would do likewise. To (white) American settlers who witnessed this ritual (as it became), the tomahawk looked like a hatchet. Hence the expression to bury the hatchet – meaning to end hostilities or make up.

A PIG'S EAR

This derives from the old proverb 'you can't make a silk purse out of a sow's ear', which dates from the sixteenth century. In other words, no matter how skilled you are, if the material you're working with is no good, you won't be able to do very much with it. So if you make a pig's ear of a job or task then you've done it badly.

_____

SOLD A PUP

This goes back to the times when people didn't buy meat – they bought animals. So you'd go to the market and buy a piglet which the salesman would put in a sack. Sometimes, if you were distracted, an unscrupulous salesman would slip a puppy into the sack instead of a piglet (puppies being worth a lot less than piglets). If you were swindled in that way you were said to have been 'sold a pup'.

_____

KEEPING UP WITH THE JONESES

The idea of 'keeping up with the Joneses' reflects on how competitive people can be – especially with their neighbours. We get the phrase from an American comic strip from a hundred years ago which ran for twenty-eight years and was adapted into books, films and even musical comedies. The 'Joneses' of the title were the neighbours of the comic strip's main characters and were spoken of but never 'seen'. The artist who devised it based it on his attempts to keep up with his own neighbours.

A SKELETON IN THE CLOSET

This dates back to the time when British law only allowed autopsies on the corpses of criminals. Given that the medical profession badly needed corpses to learn more about anatomy, there was a severe shortage of bodies. So grave diggers (known as 'resurrection men') would sometimes sell bodies to these desperate doctors who would have to keep them in a secret place to avoid detection and prosecution. Hence the phrase 'a skeleton in the closet'.

BREAK THE ICE

Before the days of motorized transport, city ports suffered during the winter because frozen rivers prevented ships from entering the city. Small ships known as icebreakers would rescue the icebound ships by breaking the ice and creating a route for them to follow. From there, it's easy to see why we might break the ice before doing business with someone.

Wonderful Wildlife Words

ANIMAL HYBRIDS

Cama, from camel and llama

Geep, from goat and sheep

Labradoodle, from Labrador Retriever and Poodle

Liger, from lion and tiger (progeny of lion and tigress)

Tigon, from tiger and lion (progeny of tiger and lioness)

Wallaroo, from wallaby and kangaroo

Wolfdog, from wolf and dog

Wolphin, from whale and dolphin

Zeedonk, from zebra and donkey

SOME GENUINE NAMES FOR
FLOWERS AND PLANTS

Love-In-Idleness

Dog's-Tooth-Grass

Old Man's Beard

Jack-Go-To-Bed-At-Noon

None So Pretty

Witches'-Butter

Gill-Over-The Ground

Devil's Snuffbox

Elephant's-Ears

THE AMPERSAND

'&' is a shortened form of the word 'and'. It's known as an ampersand which is a corruption of the words 'and, per se, and'. Here's the explanation. When people used to recite the alphabet, they'd go through the twenty-six letters and then say 'and, *per se*, and' to describe the symbol &. The words *per se* mean 'by itself'. In other words, they'd be saying, '. . . w, x, y, z, and, by itself, and'. You can see how 'and, *per se*, and' would become 'ampersand'.

Wonderful 'New' Words

Every year, *The Washington Post* holds a neologism contest, in which readers are asked to supply alternative meanings for common words. The 2013 winners were:

Abdicate: to give up all hope of ever having a flat stomach

Balderdash: a rapidly receding hairline

Coffee: the person upon whom one coughs

Circumvent: an opening in the front of boxer shorts worn by Jewish men

Esplanade: to attempt an explanation while drunk

Flabbergasted: appalled over how much weight you have gained

Flatulence: emergency vehicle that picks you up after you are run over by a steamroller

Frisbeetarianism: The belief that, when you die, your soul flies up onto the roof and gets stuck there

◆

Gargoyle: olive-flavoured mouthwash

◆

Lymph: to walk with a lisp

◆

Negligent: describes a condition in which you absentmindedly answer the door in your nightgown

◆

Oyster: a person who sprinkles his conversation with Yiddishisms

◆

Rectitude: the formal, dignified bearing adopted by proctologists

◆

Testicle: a humorous question in an exam

◆

Willy-nilly: impotent

WHERE'S IT FROM?

JAYWALKER

The word 'Jay' used to be slang for a foolish person. So when a pedestrian ignored street signs, he or she was referred to as a 'jaywalker'.

The Washington Post also asked readers to take any word from the dictionary, alter it by adding, subtracting, or changing one letter, and supply a new definition. Here were 2013's winners:

Arachnoleptic fit: the frantic dance performed just after you've accidentally walked through a spider web

★

Beelzebug: Satan in the form of a mosquito that gets into your bedroom at three in the morning and cannot be cast out

★

Bozone: the substance surrounding stupid people that stops bright ideas from penetrating. The bozone layer, unfortunately, shows little sign of breaking down in the near future

★

Cashtration: the act of buying a house, which renders the subject financially impotent for an indefinite period

★

Caterpallor: the colour you turn after finding half a grub in the fruit you're eating

★

Decafalon: the gruelling event of getting through the day consuming only things that are good for you

Dopeler effect: the tendency of stupid ideas to seem smarter when they come at you rapidly

★

Foreploy: any misrepresentation about yourself for the purpose of getting laid

★

Giraffiti: vandalism spray-painted very, very high

★

Glibido: all talk and no action

★

Hipatitis: terminal coolness

★

Ignoranus: a person who's both stupid and an asshole

★

Inoculatte: to take coffee intravenously when you are running late

★

Karmageddon: it's like, when everybody is sending off all these really bad vibes, right? And then, like, the Earth explodes and it's like, a serious bummer

★

Osteopornosis: a degenerate disease

★

Sarchasm: the gulf between the author of sarcastic wit and the person who doesn't get it

The Winning Word in all US National Spelling Bees

Every year, the United States holds a national spelling competition. School pupils qualify for it by winning regional heats. In the final, children are eliminated when they spell a word wrongly. The winning word is the one correctly spelled by the last child in the competition.

2013: Knaidel

2012: Guetapens

2011: Cymotrichous

2010: Stromuhr

2009: Laodicean

2008: Guerdon

2007: Serrefine

2006: Ursprache

2005: Appoggiatura

2004: Autochthonous

2003: Pococurante

2002: Prospicience

2001: Succedaneum

2000: Demarche

1999: Logorrhea

1998: Chiaroscurist

1997: Euonym

1996: Vivisepulture

1995: Xanthosis

1994: Antediluvian

1993: Kamikaze

1992: Lyceum

1991: Antipyretic

1990: Fibranne

1989: Spoliator

1988: Elegiacal

1987: Staphylococci

1986: Odontalgia

1985: Milieu

1984: Luge

1983: Purim

1982: Psoriasis

1981: Sarcophagus

1980: Elucubrate

1979: Maculature

1978: Deification

1977: Cambist

1976: Narcolepsy

1975: Incisor

1974: Hydrophyte

1973: Vouchsafe

1972: Macerate

1971: Shalloon

1970: Croissant

1969: Interlocutory

1968: Abalone

1967: Chihuahua

1966: Ratoon

1965: Eczema

1964: Sycophant

1963: Equipage

1962: Esquamulose

1961: Smaragdine

1960: Troche

1959: Cacolet

1958: Syllepsis

1957: Schappe

1956: Condominium

1955: Crustaceology

1954: Transept

1953: Soubrette

1952: Vignette

1951: Insouciant

1950: Haruspex

1949: Dulcimer

1948: Psychiatry

1947: Chlorophyll

1946: Semaphore

1943–5: No spelling bee was held

1942: Sacrilegious

1941: Initials

1940: Therapy

1939: Canonical

1938: Sanitarium

1937: Promiscuous

1936: Interning

1935: Intelligible

1934: Deteriorating

1933: Propitiatory

1932: Knack

1931: Foulard

1930: Fracas

1929: Asceticism

1928: Albumen

1927: Luxuriance

1926: Abrogate

1925: Gladiolus

Oxymorons

Amicable Divorce
Army Intelligence
Business Ethics
Business Trip
Civil Disobedience
Civil Servant
Committee Decision
Corporate Hospitality
Crash Landing
Deafening Silence
Dry Drunk
Educated Guess
Executive Decision
Floppy Disk
Free Trade
Friendly Fire
Guest Host

Irregular Pattern
Jumbo Shrimp
Little While
Living Dead
Martial Law
Mercy Killing
Metal Woods
Microsoft Works
Operator Service
Paid Volunteer
Same Difference
Student Teacher
Sweet Sorrow
Virtual Reality
Working Holiday
Working Lunch

WHERE'S IT FROM?

HAIR SHIRT

To wear a hair shirt means to punish yourself excessively for imagined faults. Thomas Becket, a twelfth-century Archbishop of Canterbury, wore a real shirt made of hair which he refused to take off. After he died – murdered on the wishes (if not the orders) of King Henry II – they found his hair shirt was crawling with lice.

OK

There are several different possibilities. In no particular order, they are:

1. Obediah Kelly – a US railroad freight agent who marked his initials on important papers to show that everything was in order.

2. *Okeh* – the Choctaw Indian word for 'yes'.

3. 'Orl Korect' or 'Oll Korrect' – nineteenth-century US President Andrew Jackson's folksy way of expressing himself (apparently using 'comical' initials was terribly popular in the 1830s) which led to him being known as OK Jackson.

4. Old Kinderhook – President Jackson's successor, Martin Van Buren, joined in the 'OK' fun and used the initials to refer to his home town of Kinderhook.

5. *Olla Kalla* – the Greek expression for 'all is good'.

6. *O Ke* – in Mandingo (a West African language) means 'all right'.

7. *Wav Kay* – in Wolof (a language of Senegal and Gambia) means 'yes indeed'.

8. *Omnia Correctes* – in Latin means 'all is correct'.

9. Och Aye – in Scottish means 'oh yes'.

10. Oc – is derived from the Latin affirmative *hoc*.

What is certain is that US President Van Buren popularized the expression so that by the 1840s it was in wide usage.

Palindromes

A palindrome is a word or sentence that reads the same backwards or forwards.

- A Santa lived as a devil at NASA
- A Toyota
- Denim axes examined
- Dennis and Edna sinned
- Desserts, I stressed
- Did Hannah say as Hannah did?
- Live not on evil
- Madam, I'm Adam
- Never odd or even
- Nurse, I spy gypsies – run!
- Sex at noon taxes
- Step on no pets
- Too hot to hoot

WHERE'S IT FROM?

RUGBY TRY

When rugby first started, games were won by kicking goals between the posts. Touching the ball down in the opposition's in-goal area (or 'try zone' as it's called now) didn't actually win you any points. Instead, it earned you the chance to 'try' to kick the ball through the posts – what we now call a conversion.

Pangrams

A pangram is a sentence that uses every letter of the alphabet at least once.

- The quick brown fox jumps over a lazy dog
- A very bad quack might jinx zippy fowls
- A wizard's job is to vex chumps quickly in fog
- Bawds jog, flick quartz, vex nymph
- Big fjords vex quick waltz nymph
- Brick quiz whangs jumpy veldt fox
- Bright vixens jump; dozy fowl quack
- DJs flock by when MTV ax quiz prog
- Few black taxis drive up major roads on quiet hazy nights
- Foxy diva Jennifer Lopez wasn't baking my quiche
- Jackdaws love my big sphinx of quartz
- Pack my box with five dozen liquor jugs
- Public junk dwarves quiz mighty fox
- Six plump boys guzzling cheap raw vodka quite joyfully
- The five boxing wizards jump quickly
- Vexed nymphs go for quick waltz job
- Waxy and quivering, jocks fumble the pizza
- Wet squid's inky haze veils sex of jumping crab
- Xylophone wizard begets quick jive form

How to Use Words Properly

Steer well clear of clichés; give them a wide berth.

❋

Do not be redundant; do not use more words to express an idea or concept than you really need to use.

❋

All verbs *has* to agree with subjects.

❋

Always avoid annoying alliteration.

❋

Be specific, more or less.

❋

Parenthetical remarks (however pertinent) are (almost certainly) superfluous.

❋

Complete sentences only, please.

❋

The passive voice is to be avoided.

❋

Foreign words and phrases are *de trop*.

❋

Delete commas, that are, not necessary.

One should *never* generalize.

✳

Eschew ampersands & abbreviations, etc.

✳

Analogies in writing are like pyjamas on a cat.

✳

Never use a big word where a diminutive expression
would suffice.

✳

Eliminate quotations. As Ralph Waldo Emerson said,
'I hate quotations.'

✳

A mixed metaphor, even one that flies like a bird, should
be given its marching orders.

✳

Who needs rhetorical questions?

✳

Exaggeration is a million times worse than understatement.

✳

Proofread carefully to see if you any words out.

The Most Beautiful Words in the English Language?

In 2004, to mark its seventieth anniversary, the British Council polled 7,000 people in forty-six countries to ask them what they considered to be the most beautiful words in the English language. There was also an online poll that attracted over 35,000 votes. Here are the results:

mother	grace	sentiment
passion	rainbow	cosmopolitan
smile	blue	bubble
love	sunflower	pumpkin
eternity	twinkle	banana
fantastic	serendipity	lollipop
destiny	bliss	if
freedom	lullaby	bumblebee
liberty	sophisticated	giggle
tranquillity	renaissance	paradox
peace	cute	delicacy
blossom	cosy	peek-a-boo
sunshine	butterfly	umbrella
sweetheart	galaxy	kangaroo
gorgeous	hilarious	flabbergasted
cherish	moment	hippopotamus
enthusiasm	extravaganza	gothic
hope	aqua	coconut

smashing	oi	fuselage
whoops	gazebo	zing
tickle	hiccup	gum
loquacious	hodgepodge	hen night
flip-flop	shipshape	
smithereens	explosion	

WHERE'S IT FROM?

THE SILENT 'B' IN WORDS LIKE 'LAMB' AND 'DOUBT'

By the fifteenth century, most English words had their origins in either Anglo-Saxon or French (after the Norman Invasion of 1066). The word 'doubt', for example, was then spelled 'dout' as it had come from the French word *doute*. 'Aha,' said the scholars who wanted to revive the classical world of the Greeks and the Romans, 'this word has its origins in Latin, it comes from the word *dubitare*. Let's add a "b" to reflect that (and to show how clever we are).' And that's what they did. 'Dout' became 'doubt' and other words suffered the same fate. So much so that our language is now haunted by silent letters:

The g is always silent in words like 'gnarl' and 'sign'.

The h is always silent in words like 'ghost' and 'ghastly'.

The k is always silent in words like 'knee' and 'knowledge'.

The silent 'w' before words like 'wrong' and 'wrestle' is a legacy from the days when the 'w' in these words was pronounced because Old English was based on Old German.

Words of Yiddish or Jewish Origin

Bagel: a ring-shaped bread roll
(ideal with 'lox' – see below)

◆

Chutzpah: cheek, audacity, effrontery

◆

Glitch: a minor malfunction

◆

Klutz: clumsy person

◆

Kvetch: complain, gripe

◆

Lox: smoked salmon

◆

Mensch: decent human being

◆

Nosh: snack

◆

Schlep: to drag or carry (something);
make a tedious journey

Schmaltz: excessive sentimentality

◆

Schmendrik: fool

◆

Schmooze: chat, butter up

◆

Schmutter: (cheap) clothing

◆

Shtick: comic theme; defining habit

◆

Spiel: sales pitch

◆

Tush: bottom; butt

WHERE'S IT FROM?

WIKI (AS FOUND IN WIKIPEDIA AND WIKILEAKS)
A 'wiki' is a website that uses collaborative software to allow users – i.e. members of the public – to create and edit web pages. Ward Cunningham developed the first Wiki and launched it on the internet in 1995. He chose the term 'Wiki' after riding on the Wiki Wiki Shuttle buses that run between the terminals at Honolulu International Airport. In Hawaiian, *wiki* means 'quick' and *wiki wiki* means 'very quick'.

A Word to the Wise 2
Did you know ...

The word **quiz** was allegedly invented in 1780 by a Dublin theatre manager, who bet he could introduce a new word of no meaning into the language within twenty-four hours.

*

Alice in Wonderland author Lewis Carroll invented the word **chortle** – a combination of **chuckle** and **snort**.

*

Dr Seuss invented the word **nerd** for his 1950 book *If I Ran the Zoo.*

*

The word **queueing** is the only English word with five consecutive vowels.

*

Wedlock is derived from the Old English words for pledge (***wed***) and action (***lac***).

*

The shortest English word that contains the letters **A, B, C, D, E,** and **F** is **feedback**.

*

The Sanskrit word for **war** means **desire for more cows**.

Dixie is derived from the French word for 10 – *dix* – and was first used by a New Orleans bank that issued French-American $10 bills. Later the word expanded to represent the whole of the southern states of the US.

✵

SOS doesn't stand for 'Save Our Ship' or 'Save Our Souls' – it was chosen by a 1908 international conference on Morse Code because the letters 'S' and 'O' were easy to remember. 'S' is dot dot dot, 'O' is dash dash dash.

The word **freelance** comes from a knight whose **lance** was **free** for hire.

The word **corduroy** comes from the French *cord du roi* or **cloth of the king**.

✵

Afghanistan, Kirghistan and **Tuvalu** are the only countries with three consecutive letters in their names.

✵

Resign has two opposed meanings depending on its pronunciation: 'to quit' and 'to sign again'.

✵

Underground and **underfund** are the only two words in the English language that begin and end with the letters 'und'.

The Chinese ideogram for **trouble** shows two women living under one roof.

✻

Only four words in the English language end in **-dous**: **tremendous**, **horrendous**, **hazardous** and **stupendous**.

✻

United Arab Emirates is the longest name of a country consisting of alternating vowels and consonants.

WHERE'S IT FROM?

CUPCAKES

There are two kinds of cupcake:

One type got its name from the fact that the cakes were baked in individual pottery cups. These cupcakes are the ones we know today: any small cake that's about the size of a teacup.

The other kind of cupcake or, as it was known, 'cup cake' referred to a cake whose ingredients were measured using a standard-sized cup, instead of being weighed. So a '1234 cup cake' would have been made up of four ingredients: one cup of butter, two cups of sugar, three cups of flour, and four eggs.

It's interesting to compare these cakes based on a measure of volume (e.g. a cup) with cakes based on a measure of weight – like a pound cake.

Things That Are Not What They Seem

Rice paper contains not a grain of rice

★

French fries originated in Belgium not France

★

Great Danes come from Germany not Denmark

Ten-gallon hats
hold only about
six pints of water

Koala bears aren't bears, they're marsupials

★

Mountain goats aren't goats, they're small antelopes

★

Fireflies aren't flies, they're beetles

★

The **funny bone** isn't a bone, it's a nerve

Jackrabbits aren't rabbits, they're hares

★

Shooting stars are meteors

★

Prairie dogs aren't dogs, they're rodents

★

Guinea pigs aren't pigs and nor are they from Guinea – they're South American rodents

★

Catgut isn't made from cats, it's made from sheep

★

Lead pencils contain no lead, they contain only graphite

Glow-worms aren't worms, they're beetles

The **horned toad** isn't a toad, it's a lizard

★

Bombay duck isn't duck, it's dried fish

★

Turkish baths originated in Ancient Rome, not in Turkey

★

Silkworms aren't worms, they're caterpillars

The NATO and Pre-NATO Phonetic Alphabets

NATO

Alpha	Juliet	Sierra
Bravo	Kilo	Tango
Charlie	Lima	Uniform
Delta	Mike	Victor
Echo	November	Whiskey
Foxtrot	Oscar	X-ray
Golf	Papa	Yankee
Hotel	Quebec	Zulu
India	Romeo	

Pre-NATO*

Able	Jig	Sugar
Baker	King	Tare
Charlie	Love	Uncle
Dog	Mike	Victor
Easy	Nan	William
Fox	Oboe	X-ray
George	Peter	Yoke
How	Queen	Zebra
Item	Roger	

* As used by British and American forces in World War Two

Acronyms

BAFTA (as in the annual TV and film awards): British Academy of Film and Television Arts

❖

DAB (Radio): Digital Audio Broadcasting

❖

DEFCON: Defence readiness condition

❖

DIY: Do It Yourself (home improvements)

❖

LASER: Light Amplification by Stimulated Emission of Radiation

❖

NAAFI (military canteen): Navy, Army and Air Force Institute

❖

NATO: North Atlantic Treaty Organization

❖

PIN: Personal Identification Number

❖

QANTAS: Queensland And Northern Territory Aerial Services

QUANGO: QUasi Autonomous Non-Governmental Organization

❖

SCUBA: Self Contained Underwater Breathing Apparatus

❖

SWAT (team): Special Weapons And Tactics

❖

TARDIS (*Doctor Who*): Time And Relative Dimensions In Space

❖

TASER: Thomas A. Swift's Electric Rifle

ALTERNATIVE COMPUTER ACRONYMS

WWW: World Wide Wait

❖

EMAIL: Endure Mailshots And Idiotic Letters

❖

MICROSOFT: Most Intelligent Consumers Realize Our Software Only Fools Toddlers

❖

APPLE: Arrogance Produces Profit-Losing Entity

WINDOWS: Will Install Needless Data
On Whole System

✦

ISDN: It Still Does Nothing

✦

CD-ROM: Computer Device – Rendered
Obsolete in Months

✦

MSN: Massive Spamming Network

✦

IBM: I Blame Microsoft

WHERE'S IT FROM?

THE EXCHEQUER
(AS IN THE CHANCELLOR OF THE EXCHEQUER)

In the days before calculators, they used to do calculations
in all sorts of different ways. The place that looked after
the country's money was no different. From the twelfth
century onwards, they used a chequered cloth to make
their calculations and although this stopped in the
nineteenth century, the place where they worked had
become known as the Exchequer and this name survived
to form part of the Chancellor's title.

Mnemonics

THE ORDER OF PLANETS IN DISTANCE FROM THE SUN

Mercury, Venus, Earth, Mars, Jupiter, Saturn, Uranus, Neptune, Pluto – **M**y **V**ery **E**asy **M**ethod: **J**ust **S**et **U**p **N**ine **P**lanets

❊

COLOURS OF THE RAINBOW

Red, Orange, Yellow, Green, Blue, Indigo, Violet – **R**ichard **O**f **Y**ork **G**ave **B**attle **I**n **V**ain

❊

THE ORDER OF GEOLOGICAL TIME PERIODS

Cambrian, Ordovician, Silurian, Devonian, Carboniferous, Permian, Triassic, Jurassic, Cretaceous, Paleocene, Eocene, Oligocene, Miocene, Pliocene, Pleistocene, Recent – **C**ows **O**ften **S**it **D**own **C**arefully. **P**erhaps **T**heir **J**oints **C**reak? **P**ersistent **E**arly **O**iling **M**ight **P**revent **P**ainful **R**heumatism

❊

THE COUNTRIES OF CENTRAL AMERICA IN GEOGRAPHICAL ORDER

Belize, Guatemala, Honduras, Nicaragua, Costa Rica, Panama – **B**ee**G**ee's **H**en! See [C] 'er **p**ee?

THE ORDER OF MOHS HARDNESS SCALE, FROM 1 TO 10

Talc, Gypsum, Calcite, Fluorite, Apatite, Orthoclase feldspar, Quartz, Topaz, Corundum, Diamond – **T**oronto **G**irls **C**an **F**lirt, **A**nd **O**ther **Q**ueer **T**hings **C**an **D**o

THE ORDER OF SHARPS IN MUSIC

FCGDAEB – **F**ather **C**harles **G**oes **D**own **A**nd **E**nds **B**attle

THE ORDER OF NOTES TO WHICH GUITAR STRINGS
SHOULD BE TUNED

EBGDAE – **E**aster **B**unnies **G**et **D**runk **A**t **E**aster

THE ORDER OF TAXONOMY IN BIOLOGY

Kingdom, Phylum, Class, Order, Family, Genus, Species – **K**ids **P**refer **C**heese **O**ver **F**ried **G**reen **S**pinach

THE FOUR OCEANS

Indian, Arctic, Atlantic, Pacific – **I A**m **A P**erson

THE SEVEN CONTINENTS

Europe, Antarctica, Asia, Africa, Australia, North America, South America – **E**at **AN AS**pirin **AF**ter **AU**gmenting **N**oah's **S**hip

THE GREAT LAKES

Huron, Ontario, Michigan, Erie, Superior – **HOMES**

THE GREAT LAKES IN ORDER OF SIZE

Superior, Huron, Michigan, Erie, Ontario – **S**am's **H**orse **M**ust **E**at **O**ats

✧

THE CONFEDERATE STATES OF AMERICA

South Carolina, Louisiana, Georgia, North Carolina, Alabama, Arkansas, Virginia, Mississippi, Florida, Tennessee and Texas – **S**ultry **C**arol **L**anguished **G**rumpily **N**ear **C**arl, **A**lways **A**ware **V**irginal **M**en **F**requently **T**ake **T**ime

---

WHERE'S IT FROM?

NEWS AS AN ACRONYM FOR 'NORTH, EAST, WEST, SOUTH'

The news is gathered from all four corners of the world so why shouldn't it derive its name from those four corners? Unfortunately, this is almost certainly one of those explanations that occurred to people *after* the word had  already been invented. In other words, it's a 'bacronym'.

Quite simply, the word 'news' is the plural of the word 'new'. In other words, the news consists of new things that are happening. It was only later that people said, 'These are the first four lettters of the four main points of the compass: it must explain the use of the word "news".'

Scrabble

Scrabble was invented in 1931 by Alfred Butts, an unemployed American architect. Butts (who wasn't himself a good Scrabble player and admitted that the game should have had fewer 'i's) originally called the game 'Lexico'. However, both the format and the name were changed many times – later names included 'Alpha' and 'Criss Cross Words' – before the current format was established with the name Scrabble in 1948.

The game wasn't commercially successful until 1952 when the chairman of the New York department store Macy's became addicted to it on holiday. He placed a large order for the game and did a huge promotional campaign. The rest is history.

In 1954, the game took off in Britain – selling a phenomenal 4.5 million sets. Today, an estimated fifty-three per cent of homes in Britain have a set. Scrabble is currently produced in thirty different languages – from Afrikaans to Hebrew, from Japanese and English to Malay. In total, more than 100 million games have been sold in 121 countries.

WHERE'S IT FROM?

BERSERK

This is used to mean 'mad' or 'out of control'. It comes from the Norse for 'bare shirt' because the Vikings went into battle bare-chested – whatever the weather – and fought like madmen.

MORE SCRABBLE FACTS

Celebrity Scrabble fans include Brad Pitt, Jennifer Aniston, Will Smith, Robbie Williams, Dame Elizabeth Taylor, Kylie Minogue, Madonna, Sting and Mel Gibson.

The highest number of points that can be achieved on the first go (when there are no other letters on the board) is 126 – using the word QUARTZY or the word SQUEEZY. Don't forget that there is a fifty-point bonus for using all seven letters in one go.

The highest score achieved for one word in a competition (i.e. when other people were watching) was 392 for CAZIQUES down two triple word scores, by Dr Karl Khoshnaw from Twickenham.

As all good Scrabble players know, there are 109 permissible two-letter words. These include 'Jo' (a northern sweetheart), 'Ka' (an attendant spirit), 'Xi' (a letter in the Greek alphabet) and 'Qi' (derived from Chinese, meaning life force).

WHERE'S IT FROM?

CHUNDER

This comes from the convict ships which were sent to Australia in the nineteenth century. When seasick convicts were about to throw up, they would shout 'Watch under!' as a warning to anyone unfortunate enough to be below them at the time. It's not hard to see how 'watch under' became 'chunder'.

THE MOST VALUABLE WORDS YOU CAN MAKE IN SCRABBLE

WORD MEANING AND SCORE
(+ bonus of fifty for using all seven letters)

QUIZZIFY*: To cause to look odd [31]

(**NB:** If this were stretched across two triple word scores, it would total 419 points – including the fifty-point bonus and the double letter bonus for the Z)

●

WHIPJACK: A whining beggar who pretends to be a sailor [29]

●

HIGHJACK: Alternative spelling of hijack [28]

●

JUMBOIZE: To enlarge a ship by adding a prefabricated section [28]

●

BEZIQUES: Plural of card game [28]

●

CAZIQUES: West Indian chiefs [28]

QUIZZERY*: Collection of quizzes or information pertaining to quizzes [28]

●

TZADDIQS: In Judaism, leaders or persons of extraordinary piety [28]

●

VIZCACHA: South American burrowing rodent of heavy build [27]

●

ZAMBUCKS: New Zealand or Australian colloquial term for members of St John Ambulance Brigade [27]

* Indicates that the second Z is a blank

WHERE'S IT FROM?

BLOGGERS

It was an American blogger – one Jorn Barger – who set the blog rolling when he started what he called a 'weblog' in 1997 on the basis that he was 'logging the web'. Almost immediately, another American (Peter Merholz) broke the word 'weblog' into 'we blog' and later just 'blog'. From blog to blogger was inevitable.

Expressions We Get From Baseball

Ballpark figure – approximate number

Cover all the bases – ensure safety

Curveball – a surprise

Double header – two contests/events held on the same day

Playing hardball (as in 'he's playing hardball with us') – uncompromising

Heavy hitter – a powerful person

Home run – a total success (opposite of strike out)

Left field (as in 'that idea came out of left field') – unusual or unexpected

Play ball – go along with something; start

Rain check (as in 'to take a rain check') – do something at a later date

Step up to the plate – to rise to the occasion

Three strikes and you're out – you get two chances before you're held to account

Touch base (as in 'let's touch base later') – to talk later to see that all is well

Whole new ball game – an altered situation

WHERE'S IT FROM?

BIRDIE

The term 'birdie' for one under par in golf (i.e. getting the ball in the hole in one shot less than most other golfers would), comes from a hole played by three American golfers at the Atlantic City Country Club in 1899. One of the players' balls hit a bird in flight on his second shot and landed inches from the cup. He putted in his third shot on the par-four hole and he and his friends decided that there should be a name for his achievement . . . and that name would be a birdie.

79

The Meaning Behind the Days of the Week

People have always needed to distinguish the different days of the week. True, in times past, every day was exactly the same – apart from the Sabbath day of rest – but, even then, someone might need to arrange to meet someone else in a few days' time. So it made sense to give names to the days.

We've inherited three of the names for our days from the Old English, three from the Norse and just one from the Romans:

Sunday is from the Old English *sunnandaeg*, meaning 'day of the sun'.

Monday is from the Old English *monandaeg*, or 'day of the moon'.

Tuesday is from the Old English *tiwesdaeg*, for the Norse god of combat.

Wednesday is from *wodnesdaeg*, after the supreme Norse god Woden.

Thursday is from *thorsdaeg*, after the Norse god of thunder, Thor.

Friday is from *frigedaeg*, after Frige, the Norse goddess of beauty, wife of Woden.

Saturday is named after *Saturn*, the Roman god of agriculture and the harvest.

It's interesting to compare and contrast the names of the days of the week in English and French. Whereas we have just one day named after a Roman god (Saturday), the French have several: they call Tuesday *mardi* (Mars's Day), Wednesday *mercredi* (Mercury's Day), Thursday *jeudi* (Jupiter's Day) and Friday *vendredi* (Venus's Day). As for Monday, we're all agreed that it's the day of the moon: we call it Monday and they call it *lundi* (the French word for moon is *lune*).

WHERE'S IT FROM?

AIN'T

Although it's almost always used as slang, there is one example where it's not only acceptable but also absolutely correct and that is as a contraction of the words 'am not'. In other words, wherever you would use the words 'am not' or 'am I not', you should use the word 'ain't' instead.

Take the following expression: 'I'm a good person, aren't I?'

That's incorrect, it should be 'I'm a good person, ain't I?' Why? Because 'aren't I' is a contraction of 'are not I'. Well, you don't say, 'I are a good person', do you? So you shouldn't say, 'I'm a good person, are not I?' However, 'I'm a good person, ain't I?' works because it's a quicker way of saying, 'I'm a good person, am not I' and that is absolutely correct.

Wrong Words

MALAPROPISMS

The word malapropism is derived from a character named Mrs Malaprop in the 1775 play, *The Rivals* by Richard Brinsley Sheridan. To great comic effect, Mrs Malaprop misuses words so that they don't have the meaning she intends, but sound similar to words that do. Mrs Malaprop malapropisms include: 'Sure, if I *reprehend* any thing in this world it is the use of my *oracular* tongue, and a nice *derangement* of *epitaphs*!' and '*illiterate* him quite from your memory'. However, Sheridan wasn't breaking new ground. William Shakespeare's Constable Dogberry in *Much Ado About Nothing* was clearly a blood ancestor of Mrs M: 'Our watch, sir, have indeed *comprehended* two *auspicious* persons.'

Many of us are unfortunate enough to unwittingly employ malapropisms in real life. The Australian politician, Tony Abbott, is no exception. 'No one,' he once told a party conference, 'however smart, however well educated, however experienced is the *suppository* of all wisdom.' While we're on the subject of 'repository' misspoken as 'suppository' . . . It was once reported in *New Scientist* that an office worker had described a colleague as 'a vast *suppository* of information' (rather than a *repository* or *depository*). The worker then apologized for his 'Miss-Marple-ism' (i.e. *malapropism*). The magazine suggested this was possibly the first time someone had uttered a malapropism for the word *malapropism* itself.

MONDEGREENS

A mondegreen is a misheard song lyric. There's no doubt about it, one of the most embarrassing things in the world is when you're caught singing the wrong words to a song. A friend had to explain that the Neil Diamond song 'Forever in Blue Jeans' wasn't 'Reverend Blue Jeans' and that Chaka Khan sings 'I'm Every Woman' and not 'Climb Every Woman'.

Over the past few years, I've taken to collecting such unintentional howlers from friends, family and acquaintances. The more embarrassing the mistake, the better!

Wrong line: 'I got shoes, they're made of plywood.'

Right line: 'I got chills, they're multiplying.'

Song: 'You're The One That I Want' by John Travolta and Olivia Newton-John

♫

Wrong line: 'Beelzebub has a devil for a sideboard for me.'

Right line: 'Beelzebub has a devil put aside for me.'

Song: 'Bohemian Rhapsody' by Queen

♫

Wrong line: 'I'll never leave your pizza burnin.'

Right line: 'I'll never be your beast of burden.'

Song: 'Beast of Burden' by The Rolling Stones

Wrong line: 'Sweet dreams are made of cheese.'

Right line: 'Sweet dreams are made of this.'

Song: 'Sweet Dreams (Are Made of This)' by The Eurythmics

♫

Wrong line: 'The Dukes of Hazzard are in the classroom.'

Right line: 'No dark sarcasm in the classroom.'

Song: 'Another Brick In The Wall (Part 2)' by Pink Floyd

♫

Wrong line: 'Sweet, sweet vasectomy.'

Right line: 'Free, free, set them free.'

Song: 'If You Love Somebody Set Them Free' by Sting

♫

Wrong line: 'I can't stand gravy.'

Right line: 'Constant craving.'

Song: 'Constant Craving' by k.d. lang

♫

Wrong line: 'Accountancy is my friend.'

Right line: 'The camel you see is my friend.'

Song: 'Midnight At The Oasis' by Maria Muldaur

♫

Wrong line: 'She's got electric boobs.'

Right line: 'She's got electric boots.'

Song: 'Bennie And The Jets' by Elton John

Wrong line: 'You take a piece of meat with you.'

Right line: 'You take a piece of me with you.'

Song: 'Everytime You Go Away' by Paul Young

♫

Wrong line: 'They sent you a tie-clasp.'

Right line: 'They said you was high class.'

Song: 'Hound Dog' by Elvis Presley

♫

Wrong line: 'Bring out the arms of Nemo.'

Right line: 'Break out the arms and ammo.'

Song: 'Something In The Air' by Thunderclap Newman

♫

Wrong line: 'Right on the pee stain.'

Right line: 'Ride on the peace train.'

Song: 'Peace Train' by Cat Stevens

♫

Wrong line: 'They call her a tramp.'

Right line: 'We're caught in a trap.'

Song: 'Suspicious Minds' by Elvis Presley

♫

Wrong line: 'Now I'll never dance with her mother.'

Right line: 'Now I'll never dance with another.'

Song: 'I Saw Her Standing There' by The Beatles

85

Wrong line: 'I believe in milk and cows.'

Right line: 'I believe in miracles.'

Song: 'You Sexy Thing' by Hot Chocolate

♫

Wrong line: 'And doughnuts make my brown eyes blue.'

Right line: 'And don't it make my brown eyes blue.'

Song: 'Don't It Make My Brown Eyes Blue' by Crystal Gayle

NEWSPAPER HEADLINES

Police Discover Crack In Australia

MAN RECOVERING AFTER FATAL ACCIDENT

SHELL FOUND ON BEACH

SPOONERISMS

A spoonerism is an error in speech in which corresponding letters are switched between two words in a phrase, for example saying, 'The Lord is a shoving leopard,' instead of 'The Lord is a loving shepherd.' It is named after the Reverend William Archibald Spooner (1844–1930), the Warden of New College, Oxford, who was notoriously prone to this mistake.

A blushing crow.

A well-boiled icicle.

Is it kisstomary to cuss the bride?

Is the bean dizzy?

Kinquering congs their titles take.

Let us drink to the queer old dean.

Someone is occupewing my pie.

Please sew me to another sheet.

That is just a half-warmed fish.

◆

The cat popped on its drawers.

◆

You have hissed all my mystery lectures. You have tasted a whole worm. Please leave Oxford on the next town drain.

◆

You were fighting a liar in the quadrangle.

GREAT MISQUOTATIONS

'I never said I want to be alone,
(I only said I want to be left alone.')
GRETA GARBO

★

'A little knowledge is a dangerous thing.'
('A little learning is a dangerous thing.')
ALEXANDER POPE

★

'Money is the root of all evil.'
('For the love of money is the root of all evil.')
THE BIBLE, TIMOTHY 6:10

★

'Abandon hope, all ye who enter here.'
('Abandon all hope, you who enter.')
THE DIVINE COMEDY BY DANTE

'Hell hath no fury like a woman scorned.'
('Heaven has no rage like love to hatred turned, Nor hell a fury like a woman scorned.')
THE MOURNING BRIDE BY WILLIAM CONGREVE

★

'Come up and see me sometime.'
('Why don't you come up sometime, and see me?')
MAE WEST TO CARY GRANT IN *SHE DONE HIM WRONG*

★

'Pride goes before a fall.'
('Pride goeth before destruction and a haughty spirit before a fall.')
THE BIBLE, PROVERBS 16:18

★

'Nice guys finish last.'
('Nice Guys Finish Seventh.')
BROOKLYN DODGERS MANAGER LEO DUROCHER
SPEAKING IN THE DAYS WHEN THE NATIONAL LEAGUE
HAD SEVEN TEAMS SO SEVENTH WAS, IN FACT, LAST.

★

'Elementary, my dear Watson.'
'Elementary.'
SHERLOCK HOLMES TO DR WATSON

★

'Hubble bubble, toil and trouble.'
'Double double, toil and trouble.'
THE WITCHES IN *MACBETH* BY WILLIAM SHAKESPEARE

'To gild the lily.'
'To gild refined gold, to paint the lily.'
THE EARL OF SALISBURY IN *KING JOHN*
BY WILLIAM SHAKESPEARE

★

'Me Tarzan, you Jane.'
TARZAN AND JANE POINTED AT THEMSELVES AND EACH SAID
THEIR OWN NAME
IN *TARZAN THE APE MAN.*

★

'Et tu, Brutus?'
'Et tu, Brute?'
JULIUS CAESAR (IN THE UNLIKELY EVENT THAT
HE SAID THOSE WORDS, BRUTUS WOULD HAVE
TAKEN THE VOCATIVE).

★

'When in Rome do as the Romans do.'
'If you are at Rome, live after the Roman fashion; if you
are elsewhere, live as they do there.'
ST AMBROSE

★

'Don't look a gift horse in the mouth.'
'Never inspect the teeth of a gift horse.'
ORIGINAL PROVERB

'Discretion is the better part of valour.'
'The better part of valour is discretion.'
FALSTAFF, *KING HENRY IV, PART I*
BY WILLIAM SHAKESPEARE

★

'There's method in his madness.'
'Though this be madness, yet there is method in't.'
POLONIUS, *HAMLET* BY WILLIAM SHAKESPEARE

★

'In the future, everybody will be famous for fifteen minutes.'
('In the future, there won't be any more stars.
TV will be so accessible that everybody will be
a star for fifteen minutes.')
ANDY WARHOL

WHERE'S IT FROM?

PRIVATE EYES

In 1925, the American Pinkerton Agency – probably the most famous private detective agency in the world – ran an advertising campaign which featured a large picture of an eye and the slogan 'We never sleep'. As a direct result of this advertising, private detectives became known as private eyes.

GOOGLE

Google was founded by Larry Page and Sergey Brin in 1996 while they were studying at Stanford University, California. It wasn't something they did in their spare time, it was actually a research project.

Back then, conventional search engines ranked results by counting how many times the search terms appeared on the page. The Google Guys (as they became known) thought there was a better way of doing it: they made sure that when you entered a search term, you didn't get the websites with the most times that the search term was mentioned – you got the sites that made the most sense to you, that was of the most value to you. And why? Because these were the sites, ranked in descending order of relevance, that all the previous people who had ever used your search terms had decided were the most useful to them. In other words, you were benefiting from cumulative knowledge and usage.

Page and Brin originally nicknamed their new search engine 'BackRub' because the system checked backlinks to estimate the importance of a site. Later, they changed the name to Google, a play on the word 'googol', which is the number one followed by one hundred zeros. They picked this to show that the search engine would provide large quantities of information for lots of people.

The domain name for Google was registered in 1997 and the company Google was launched the following year.

Golden Bull Award Winners

The winners of 2013's Golden Bull awards for the worst examples of gobbledygook – as 'presented' by the Plain English Campaign:

An open seminar at the University of Essex Centre for Psychoanalytic Studies entitled: *Between the unspeakable and the speculum: Poetry and Psychoanalysis*

> This paper will be a reflection on what endures and on the archaeology of utterance – an archaeology that is intimately connected to castration. As a Symbolic artefact poetry stands between the darkness of the unknowable – Freud's navel – and Lacan's mirror of semblance in which false architectures of the self, emerge as a parody of the truth.

Response from the tax office after an attempt to email them a file:

> The submission of this document has failed due to departmental specific business logic in the Body tag. Your submission contains an unrecognized namespace.

From a letter sent by Alliance Trust Savings:

> How will I be impacted? We have confirmed with the Fund Managers that the rebate paying share classes you are invested in, listed overleaf, have an equivalent within the 'clean share' class. The new share class has a lower or equal net AMC to the fund that you are currently invested in and so you will either pay the same, or less, than you did previously when taking any previous rebates into account.

From a letter from the Department of Energy and Climate Change:

> The second part consists of an Occupancy Assessment (OA) that adjusts the standardized EPC estimates based on information about the occupants . . . GDARS build upon the information in the EPC by incorporating additional information gathered from the OA about how the occupants in the property actually use energy . . . I hope this is helpful.

Celtic carvery and alehouse 'bar manager/manageress' job advertisement:

Job Purpose

Provides beverages by procuring beverage ingredients.

Duties

Accomplishes bar human resource objectives by recruiting, selecting, orienting, training, assigning, scheduling, coaching, counselling, and disciplining employees. Achieves bar operational objectives by contributing information and analysis to functional strategic plans and reviews. Plans beer, wine, and spirits drink menus by researching mixology techniques.

Chief investment officer about the sale of a business park:

The sale is very much in line with our ongoing focus on recycling capital out of assets at the appropriate time in the cycle in order to crystallize gains from higher value uses and redeploy into other profitable growth opportunities in our core markets.

SUPERCALIFRAGILISTICEXPIALIDOCIOUS

When the film *Mary Poppins* came out in 1964, the song 'Supercalifragilisticexpialidocious' was an instant hit with everyone except a couple of songwriters who'd written a song called 'Supercalafajaistickespeealadojus' fifteen years earlier and had actually shown it to Disney (the film's producers). They – not unreasonably – brought a legal case against the composers of 'Supercalifragilisticexpialidocious' for several million dollars. However, they lost because, after listening to several witnesses, the judge decided that the word – or words like it – had been in use for years before either song had been written.

No one had any idea what the word meant – if anything – with the composers of the *Mary Poppins* song claiming that it was just 'a very long word that had been passed down in many variations through many generations of kids. The word was first coined in 1918, and was supposed to be even bigger and harder to say than *antidisestablishmentarianism*.

Enough to End It All?

In 1927, Edwin Wakeman of Manchester committed suicide leaving this note: 'I married a widow with a grown daughter. My father fell in love with my stepdaughter and married her – thus becoming my son-in-law. My stepdaughter became my stepmother because she was my father's wife. My wife gave birth to a son, who was, of course, my father's brother-in-law, and also my uncle, for he was the brother of my stepmother. My father's wife became the mother of a son, who was, of course, my brother, and also my grandchild, for he was the son of my stepdaughter. Accordingly, my wife was my grandmother, because she was my stepmother's mother. I was my wife's husband and grandchild at the same time. And, as the husband of a person's grandmother is his grandfather, I am my own grandfather.'

WHERE'S IT FROM?

DOGSBODY

This has its roots in the British Navy of the nineteenth century. One of the ghastly foods that British sailors were given to eat was pease pudding (a sort of dried pea concoction). The sailors, however, called it dog's body – possibly because of the shape of the bag that the peas came in. Over time, the sort of sailor who had to eat this food and the food's nickname became one. Eventually, the word dogsbody became used to describe any underling who always gets the worst jobs.

Unfortunate (Genuine) Website Addresses

www.expertsexchange.com (Experts Exchange)
www.ipanywhere.com (Internet Protocol Anywhere)
www.childrenswear.co.uk (Childrens Wear)
www.speedofart.com (Speed of Art)
www.dicksonweb.com (Dickson Web)
www.teacherstalk.com (Teachers Talk)
www.auctionshit.com (Auctions Hit)
www.gotahoe.com (Go Tahoe)
www.goredfoxes.com (Marist Red Foxes)
www.choosespain.com (Choose Spain)
www.penisland.net (Pen Island)
www.whorepresents.com (Who Represents)
www.powergenitalia.com (Power Gen Italia)

WHERE'S IT FROM?

GERMAN MEASLES

This has nothing to do with Germany and everything to do with how words get changed over the years. In this instance, the word 'German' is a corruption of the word 'germane' – meaning alike or akin. German Measles was once known as Germane (to) Measles, the viral illness to which it is related. From there, it was a short journey to its current name (although the medical name is, of course, Rubella).

The Funniest Joke in the World?

In 2002, after much research, British scientists identified what they called 'The Funniest Joke in the World'. Here it is:

A couple of New Jersey hunters are out in the woods when one of them falls to the ground. He doesn't seem to be breathing, his eyes are rolled back in his head. The other guy whips out his mobile phone and calls the emergency services. He gasps to the operator: 'My friend is dead! What can I do?' The operator, in a calm, soothing voice, says: 'Just take it easy. I can help. First, let's make sure he's dead.' There is a silence, then a shot is heard. The guy's voice comes back on the line. He says: 'OK, now what?'

WHERE'S IT FROM?

PUNCH

The drink punch derives from the Hindi word *panch* meaning 'five' as the drink was made from five different ingredients: spirits, sugar, lemon juice, water, and spices. There is an alternative explanation – that it may have derived from a *puncheon*, a cask holding 72 gallons, from which a punch bowl could be made. But the former is much more likely.

A boxing punch comes from the word 'pounce' – meaning 'swoop' or 'lunge'.

Bingo!

Some of the extraordinary expressions traditionally associated with bingo numbers:

1 Kelly's eye	**30** Burlington Bertie
2 One little duck	**39** Those famous steps
5 Man alive	**44** Droopy drawers
9 Doctor's orders	**55** Snakes alive
11 Legs eleven	**56** Was she worth it?
16 Never been kissed	**57** Heinz varieties
22 Two little ducks	**59** Brighton line
25 Duck and dive	**66** Clickety click
26 Bed and breakfast	**88** Two fat ladies
27 Little duck with a crutch	**90** Top of the shop

WHERE'S IT FROM?

SCAPEGOAT

This goes back to Biblical times when people would bring two goats to a sacrificial altar. One goat would be slain but the other – said to carry the sins of the congregation – was allowed to escape. Thus, the word 'scapegoat'.

Medical Expressions Used in Hospitals

Ash Cash: money paid for signing cremation forms

✚

Ash Point: where you collect the Ash Cash

✚

Code Brown: incontinence-related emergency

✚

Cold Tea Sign: the several cups of cold tea on the bedside cabinet beside a geriatric patient indicating that he/she is deceased

✚

Crumblie: a geriatric patient

✚

Departure Lounge: geriatric ward

✚

Digging For Worms: varicose vein surgery

✚

Eternal Care: intensive care

✚

Guessing Tube: stethoscope

Handbag Positive: an old lady lying in her hospital bed clutching her handbag, indicating that she's confused and disorientated

House Red: blood

Sieve: a doctor who admits every patient he sees

Treat 'n' Street: quick patient turnaround

Wall: a doctor who resists admitting patients at all costs

NEWSPAPER HEADLINES

EU Must Unite On Drugs

BLIND WOMAN GETS NEW KIDNEY FROM DAD SHE HASN'T SEEN IN YEARS

MAN STRUCK BY LIGHTNING FACES BATTERY CHARGE

Genuine Spelling Mistakes on Twitter

Derriere
'Your dairy air looks rather ravishing from
this vantage point.'

Menopause
'So hot in the office today one of the secretaries
thought she was metal pausing.'

Cologne
'I love it when you can still smell your boyfriend's
colon on you.'

Overreact
'I always ovary act to small stuff.'

Might As Well
'If your gone hang with bitches, they minus well be
female.'

Alter Ego

'Twitter is my alter eagle.'

Aphrodisiac

'Is it true that fried oysters are an afrodezyact?'

Wounds

'Time heals all wombs.'

Corn rows

'OK, but who got corn roads in they hair?'

Self-esteem

'Ladies that fall in luv with other peoples boyfriends have low selves of steam.'

No offence

'I don't have a ugly Christmas sweater. And no a fence anyone but I'm not going to waste money and time to buy one.'

Pedestal

'Women, stop puttin these men on such a high pedal stool. Not all of them are worth it #imjustsayin.'

Ornaments

'My favourite thing to do is lay under the Christmas tree and look up at all the ordiments. It looks like an enchanted forest.'

Lactose intolerant

'I can't eat dairy anymore. I think I'm lack toast and tolerant.'

C-section

'Ladies do you prefer natural birth or sea sexion?'

WHERE'S IT FROM?

SCRUPLES

A scruple was originally a stone. It came from the Latin word *scrupulus*, meaning 'little stone'. The first recorded use of the word in the context with which we're familiar was when the Roman orator Cicero used the word in a letter to a friend to convey a sense of uneasiness or anxiety similar to the discomfort caused by having a piece of gravel in your sandal.

A Word to the Wise 3

Did you know . . .

Taramasalata (a type of Greek salad) and **Galatasaray** (the name of a Turkish football club) each have an 'a' for every other letter.

✳

The word **therein** contains thirteen words spelled with consecutive letters: the, he, her, er, here, I, there, ere, rein, re, in, therein, and herein.

✳

SWIMS is the longest word with 180-degree rotational symmetry (if you were to view it upside-down it would still be the same word and perfectly readable).

✳

Unprosperousness is the longest word in which no letter occurs only once.

✳

www as an abbreviation for **World Wide Web** has nine spoken syllables, whereas the term being abbreviated has only three spoken syllables.

✳

Ultrarevolutionaries has each vowel exactly twice.

Facetious and **Abstemious** contain the five vowels in alphabetical order.

✳

Subcontinental, uncomplimentary and **duoliteral** contain the five vowels in reverse alphabetical order.

✳

Pliers is a word with no singular form. Other such words are: **alms, cattle, eaves** and **scissors**.

The shortest sentence in the English language is *Go!*

Acceded, baggage, cabbage, defaced, effaced and **feedbag** are seven-letter words that can be played on a musical instrument.

✳

The word **dude** was coined by Oscar Wilde and his friends. It is a combination of the words **duds** and **attitude**.

✳

Princes is the only plural word which can be made singular by *adding* an s (it becomes **princess**)

✳

Hijinks is the only word in common usage with three dotted letters in a row.

Earthling is first found in print in 1593. Other surprisingly old words are **spaceship** (1894), **acid rain** (1858), **antacid** (1753), **hairdresser** (1771), **mole** (in connection with espionage, 1622, by Sir Francis Bacon), **funk** (a strong smell, 1623; a state of panic, 1743), **Milky Way** (*c.* 1384, but earlier in Latin) and **Ms** (used instead of Miss or Mrs, 1949).

✳

Ewe and **You** are pronounced exactly the same, yet share no letters in common.

WHERE'S IT FROM?

THE QUESTION MARK

Punctuation is a relatively recent invention. Western and Middle Eastern languages didn't have punctuation at all and even the Assyrians and the Babylonians only put a space at the end of each sentence. Otherwise, all words just ellided into one another. This changed at the start of the seventh century when the Church, worried that priests pausing in the wrong place might convey the wrong message to their congregations, ordered dots and squiggles to be inserted into manuscripts. At the start of the ninth century, Charlemagne's court standardized punctuation and interrogatory sentences were indicated by a full stop with a tilde (~) over it. This, of course, looks a lot like our question mark and so it evolved.

Words You Might Read But Never Actually Use

Purchases
Fruiterer
Pursuance
Undertake

Confectionery
Supremo
Hereunder
Remuneration

Thereafter
Turf Accountant
Tryst

WHERE'S IT FROM?

WHY COLONEL IS PRONOUNCED 'KERNEL'

A colonel is a senior officer in the army. The word comes from the Old Italian word *colonello* (meaning commander of troops, which in turn derived from the Italian word for 'column').

Like so many words, the word came into English through the French. However – and this is where it gets more complicated – it came through as two separate words: colonel and coronel. The word 'coronel' was eventually pronounced as 'kernel'. Then someone decided that the word should be spelled the way it was originally and so it should be 'colonel'. The word was now spelled as 'colonel' but still pronounced as 'coronel' or 'kernel'.

Tongue Twisters

Six sharp smart sharks.

◆

If Stu chews shoes, should Stu choose the shoes he chews?

◆

Black back bat.

◆

Wunwun was a racehorse, Tutu was
one too. Wunwun won one race, Tutu won one too.

◆

The local yokel yodels.

A noisy noise annoys an oyster.

Red lorry, yellow lorry, red lorry, yellow lorry.

◆

A big black bug bit a big black bear, made the
big black bear bleed blood.

◆

Lesser leather never weathered wetter weather better.

◆

Cheap ship trip.

Mrs Smith's Fish Sauce Shop.

❖

Six slick slim sick sycamore saplings.

❖

Irish wristwatch.

❖

Friendly Frank flips fine flapjacks.

The sixth sick Sheik's
sixth sheep's sick.

Rory the warrior and Roger the worrier were wrongly
reared in a rural brewery.

❖

Sheena leads, Sheila needs.

❖

A box of biscuits, a batch of mixed biscuits.

❖

Eleven benevolent elephants.

❖

Is this your sister's sixth zither, sir?

❖

Scissors sizzle, thistles sizzle.

We shall surely see the sun shine soon.

◆

Three free throws.

◆

How much wood would a woodchuck chuck if a
woodchuck could chuck wood?

◆

Fred fed Ted bread and Ted fed Fred bread.

◆

Six slippery snails slid slowly seaward.

◆

Selfish shellfish.

◆

Peter Piper picked a peck of pickled peppers
Did Peter Piper pick a peck of pickled peppers?
If Peter Piper picked a peck of pickled peppers,
Where's the peck of pickled peppers Peter Piper picked?

WHERE'S IT FROM?

PRIVATE SOLDIER

This goes back to the Middle Ages when private soldiers
were hired or forced into service by the local nobleman
who had been ordered to form an army for the monarch.
They were called private soldiers because they were only
responsible for themselves – unlike their officers who
performed *public* duty by being in charge of other soldiers.

Just Think About It...

If Holly Hunter married George W. Bush,
she'd be Holly Bush.

★

If Iman married Gary Oldman,
she'd be Iman Oldman.

★

If Cherie Blair married Oliver Stone,
she'd be Cherie Stone.

★

If Minnie Driver married Alice Cooper,
she'd be Minnie Cooper.

★

If Olivia Newton-John married Wayne Newton,
then divorced him to marry Elton John,
she'd be Olivia Newton-John Newton John.

WHERE'S IT FROM?

HOBNOB

This derives from the two Old English words, *habban* ('to have') and *nabban* ('to have not') and was used to describe the practice of alternating the buying of a round of drinks. It meant having to buy a round and not having to buy a round.

Genuine Comments Made on Patients' Medical Records

'Between you and me, we ought to be able to get this lady pregnant.'

◆

'Exam of genitalia reveals that he is circus sized.'

◆

'Examination reveals a well-developed male lying in bed with his family in no distress.'

◆

'Many years ago the patient had frostbite of the right shoe.'

◆

'She has no rigors or chills but her husband says she was very hot in bed last night.'

◆

'The baby was delivered, the cord clamped and cut, and handed to the pediatrician, who breathed and cried immediately.'

◆

'The lab test indicated abnormal lover function.'

◆

'The patient has been depressed ever since she began seeing me.'

'The patient experienced sudden onset of severe shortness of breath with acute pulmonary oedema at home while having sex which gradually deteriorated in the emergency room.'

❖

'The patient is a seventy-nine-year-old widow who no longer lives with her husband.'

❖

'The patient is tearful and crying constantly. She also appears to be depressed.'

❖

'The patient lives at home with his mother, father, and pet turtle, who is presently enrolled in day care three times a week.'

❖

'The patient was to have a bowel resection. However, he took a job as stockbroker instead.'

❖

'Whilst in Casualty she was examined, X-rated and sent home.'

WHERE'S IT FROM?

HEAD HONCHO

The word 'honcho' comes from a Japanese word meaning 'squad leader' and first came into usage in the English language during the American occupation of Japan following World War Two.

Genuine Things Written by Drivers on Insurance Forms

'A bull was standing near and the fly must have tickled him as he gored my car.'

'A lamp post bumped the car, damaging it in two places.'

'A lorry backed through my windscreen into my wife's face.'

'A pedestrian hit me and went under my car.'

'An invisible car came out of nowhere, struck my car and vanished.'

'As I approached the intersection a sign suddenly appeared in a place where no sign had ever appeared before, making me unable to avoid the accident.'

'Coming home I drove into the wrong house and collided with a tree I don't have.'

'I blew my horn but it would not work as it had been stolen.'

116

'I bumped a lamp post which was obscured by pedestrians.'

'I collided with a stationary truck coming the other way.'

'I consider that neither car was to blame, but if either one was to blame, it would be the other one.'

'I didn't think the speed limit applied after midnight.'

'I had been driving for forty years when I fell asleep at the wheel and had an accident.'

'I had been learning to drive with power steering. I turned the wheel to what I thought was enough and found myself in a different direction going the opposite way.'

WHERE'S IT FROM?

SMALL BEER

In the sixteenth and seventeenth centuries, small beer was a popular drink consumed at breakfast by both adults and children. Its alcohol content was low and it was safer to drink than water because it was boiled during production, which killed off harmful bacteria.

'I had to turn the car sharper than was necessary
owing to an invisible lorry.'

'I knew the dog was possessive about the car but
I would not have asked her to drive it if I had thought
there was any risk.'

'I knocked over a man. He admitted it was his fault as he
had been run over before.'

'I pulled away from the side of the road, glanced at my
mother-in-law, and headed over the embankment.'

'I pulled into a lay-by with smoke coming from under the
hood. I realized the car was on fire so took my dog and
smothered it with a blanket.'

'I saw a slow-moving, sad-faced old gentleman as he
bounced off the roof of my car.'

'I saw her look at me twice. She appeared to be making
slow progress when we met on impact.'

'I started to turn and it was at this point I noticed a camel
and an elephant tethered at the verge. This distraction
caused me to lose concentration and hit a bollard.'

'I thought my window was down, but I found out it was up when I put my head through it.'

'I told the other idiot what he was and went on.'

'I told the police I was not injured, but upon removing my hair, I found that I had a fractured skull.'

'I was going at about 70 or 80mph when my girlfriend on the pillion reached over and grabbed my testicles so I lost control.'

'I was thrown from my car as it left the road, and was later found in a ditch by some stray cows.'

'In my attempt to kill a fly, I drove into a telephone pole.'

'My car was legally parked as it backed into the other vehicle.'

'No one was to blame for the accident but it would never have happened if the other driver had been alert.'

'She suddenly saw me, lost her head, and we met.'

'The accident happened because I had one eye on the lorry in front, one eye on the pedestrian and the other on the car behind.'

'The accident happened when the right front door of a car came round the corner without giving a signal.'

'The accident occurred when I was attempting to bring my car out of a skid by steering it into the other vehicle.'

'The pedestrian had no idea which way to run, so I ran over him.'

WHERE'S IT FROM?

HOCUS POCUS

It is thought that the word 'hocus' was taken from the genitive of the Latin word *hoax* (after all, a trick is a kind of hoax) and that the word 'pocus' was added as part of the incantation that a magician would use as part of his act. In any event, the seventeenth-century magician who popularized the expression liked it so much he changed his name to . . . Hocus Pocus.

The Origins of Expressions 2

BITE THE BULLET

This goes back to emergency surgery in wartime when there was either no anaesthetic or no time to administer any. In which case, the surgeon made patients bite down on a bullet in an attempt to distract them from the pain.

———

BUTTER UP

If you butter up someone, you're doing your utmost to please them but it's almost certainly not a pretty sight. You're being oleaginous: greasing your way into their affections and/or trying to flatter them outrageously. From a linguistic point of view, it is easy to see why words like 'buttering' and 'greasing' would come to be used in this context: the person buttering is indeed acting in an emollient – oily – way so as to make their target feel in no doubt as to their intentions.

However, there's another reason why butter (or buttering) is used: there was an ancient Indian custom that involved throwing balls of clarified butter at statues of the gods in order to seek favour. From there, you can see why we might butter up someone else to seek other favours.

———

SPILL THE BEANS

In Ancient Greece, beans were used when voting for candidates who were standing for various positions. Each candidate would be assigned a container into which the voters would place a white bean (meaning that they liked the candidate) or a black bean (signifying disapproval). Sometimes, a clumsy person would accidentally knock over the container which would 'spill the beans' and thus show how well a candidate was doing.

———

HOBSON'S CHOICE

Hobson's choice is no choice at all. Thomas Hobson (1554–1631) was the owner of a livery stable in Cambridge who rented out horses to people. He had a strict rule that customers had to take the horse nearest the stable door. If they didn't like that horse, then that was tough. So in as much as they had a choice, it was the choice of taking the horse offered to them or no horse at all. In other words, Hobson's choice: take it or leave it.

———

CLOUD NINE

This is based on terminology used by the US Weather Bureau. Clouds are divided into classes and each class is divided into nine types with level (or cloud) nine being the very highest. Such clouds can reach as high as 10,000 metres or even higher and appear as glorious white mountains in the sky. So if you were on cloud nine you'd be right at the top. And that's why it's used to describe a happy person.

FITS TO A T

Architects and other people who need to draw with extreme accuracy use T-squares to draw perfect right angles. From there, you can see why something that's spot on would be described as fitting to a T.

TO WEAR ONE'S HEART ON ONE'S SLEEVE

In the Middle Ages, on 14 February, it was the custom for young men and women to pick names out of a bowl to see who their Valentines would be for the next week. The practice was for them to wear these names (invariably written on heart-shaped pieces of paper) on their sleeves for a whole week. Therefore, wearing your heart on your sleeve became a way of saying that someone had made their feelings obvious.

STEALING THE LIMELIGHT

Limelight – which originated from the burning of lime to create a strong light – was used by lighthouses and the Victorian stage before the era of electric light. So someone who was trying to steal or hog the limelight was thrusting themselves into the middle of the stage at the expense of the other actors.

PYRRHIC VICTORY

A Pyrrhic victory is one in which you win but only at huge cost. In other words, it's a win in name only as it has all the hallmarks of a defeat. It is named after Pyrrhus, the King of Epirus who won the batttle of Asculum in 279 BC but he lost all of his officers and most of his best men in what we would now call a Pyrrhic victory.

Nowadays, we use the expression for everything from politics to sport. So if, for example, a football team wins a match but suffers terrible injuries, it could be described as a Pyrrhic victory.

———

KICK THE BUCKET

When a large animal was being killed at a slaughterhouse, a bucket would be placed under it while it was positioned on a pulley. Sometimes the animal would kick out during the process and so it would literally kick the bucket before being killed.

IN A NUTSHELL

It's all thanks to a sixteenth-century English calligrapher named Peter Bales who was able to write in such small letters that it was said of him that he could write a Bible small enough to fit into a walnut shell. From that, we get the expression 'in a nutshell' to cover any example of a concise argument or point.

AS HAPPY AS A CLAM

It's important to know the rest of this saying. It should be 'as happy as a clam at high tide'. Why? Because clams are only harvested when the tide is out and so when it's high tide, they're safe and therefore happy.

———

BREAK A LEG

One can see why superstitious actors wouldn't want people to say 'good luck' as it's tempting fate. But why invite them to break their legs? There's a two-fold explanation: firstly, it's a form of reverse superstition (i.e. if good luck is tempting fate then wish them bad luck) and secondly, it's a subtle way of saying that you hope the actor will be down on one knee at the end of the performance, bowing down before an appreciative audience – and, in olden days, picking up tips thrown on to the stage by grateful spectators.

———

BARKING UP THE WRONG TREE

This comes from raccoon hunting. Dogs were used to hunt raccoons by following their scent. When they found one, they would stop at the bottom and bark at the tree trunk. However, because raccoons are nocturnal, hunting took place in the dark and sometimes the dogs would bark at the bottom of the wrong tree . . .

FACING THE MUSIC

This goes back to the days when army court martials (or, as these trials of soldiers should technically be known in the plural, 'courts martial') were even more formal than they are today. As the commanding officer read out the charges against the soldier to be tried, an army drummer would drum by his side. The soldier on trial would therefore be 'facing the music'. So if a soldier – or later, as the saying became more widely used, a civilian – was going to be doing something risky or even illegal, he would talk about 'facing the music' if he was caught.

Interestingly, another expression is associated with this one. If someone is fitted up – i.e. accused of doing something bad that they didn't do – then they would be facing 'drummed-up' charges or the case could be described as 'drummed up'.

———

CHANCE ONE'S ARM

There are two possible explanations. The first is that it comes from boxing. When a boxer extends his fist to hit his opponent, he is leaving himself vulnerable to counter-attack. In that way, he's chancing his arm.

The other (earlier) possibility is that it refers to a soldier – specifically a corporal or a sergeant – doing something that might bring him into trouble and lead to him being demoted and therefore having his stripes removed from the arm of his tunic. In that way he would be chancing his arm.

TOO MANY TO SHAKE A STICK AT

Shepherds would control their sheep by shaking their staffs (large sticks) to indicate where the animals should go. When farmers had more sheep than they could control, it was obvious that they had too many to shake a stick at.

LET ONE'S HAIR DOWN

In seventeenth- and eighteenth-century Paris, members of the nobility were obliged to wear elaborate hairdos – stacked preposterously high – which took several hours to prepare. At the end of a long day's intriguing and ingratiating at the Palace of Versailles, they'd go home to relax and the first thing they'd do would be to let their hair down.

BUFFS

Anyone who's an expert on – or an enthusiast for – something (maybe films or stamps) is described as a buff. In nineteenth-century New York, firefighters noticed that whenever they attended a fire, they would be followed by men who were eager to watch them. Because these men wore buffalo fur to protect them against the cold, the firefighters started calling them 'buffalos' or 'buffs' for short.

TO TAKE A RAIN CHECK

In the US, a rain check was offered to people who had tickets to a baseball game that was rained off. They would be given a rain check which was a ticket for a game at a later date.

COOL AS A CUCUMBER

There's a good reason why cucumber is used as the epitome of cool and it's entirely down to the fact that however hot or cold the weather is, the middle of a cucumber – its core – is usually some 11° C (20° F) colder than its outside temperature.

GETTING ON ONE'S HIGH HORSE

It comes from olden times when a person's rank was determined by the height of their horse (and a high horse indicated a superior person).

TO KNOW ONE'S ONIONS

A myth has grown up that this is a reference to a British lexicographer, one Charles Talbut Onions, who worked on the *Oxford English Dictionary* and was so knowledgeable that his name became a byword for expertise. In fact, it comes from the US where it was just one of many such expressions that included 'knows his apples', 'knows his oats' etc.

A FEATHER IN ONE'S CAP

This comes from Native North American people who would reward warriors who killed their enemies, or hunters who killed lots of animals, with feathers to wear in their ceremonial headdress. From here, it's easy to see why a feather in the cap would have been used to describe any achievement.

BRING HOME THE BACON

In sixteenth-century Europe, being able to afford pork was considered a sign of great wealth. So a man who could 'bring home the bacon' was more than providing for his family. When he entertained friends, he would cut off a piece of bacon or pork and give it to them to eat. They would sit around and (this is where this saying is derived from) 'chew the fat'.

COLD TURKEY

It used to be thought that the skin of a person going through drug withdrawal would change – becoming harder and covered with goose bumps, like the skin of a plucked turkey.

GOING ROUND THE BEND

This derives from operators stationed on Telegraph Island who were desperate to escape to India by sailing round the bend in the Strait of Hormuz.

———

NO STRINGS ATTACHED

Traditionally, cloth merchants have always marked any flaws in their cloth with a tiny white string. Flawless cloth would be ordered by requesting 'no strings attached'.

———

RULE OF THUMB

This derives from the old English law that stipulated you couldn't beat your wife with anything wider than your thumb.

WHERE'S IT FROM?

NOSY PARKER

Matthew Parker was Archbishop of Canterbury in the sixteenth century. He had a very long nose and was extremely inquisitive – hence 'nosy parker'.

School Daze

GENUINE METAPHORS TAKEN FROM ENGLISH ESSAYS

'The plan was simple, like my brother Phil. But unlike Phil, this plan just might work.'

✳

'The young fighter had a hungry look, the kind you get from not eating for a while.'

'His thoughts tumbled in his head, making and breaking alliances like underpants in a tumble dryer.'

'The little boat gently drifted across the pond exactly the way a bowling ball wouldn't.'

✳

'Her hair glistened in the rain like nose hair after a sneeze.'

✳

'Her eyes were like two brown circles with big black dots in the centre.'

✳

'Her vocabulary was as bad as, like, whatever.'

'He was as tall as a six-foot-three-inch tree.'

❋

'John and Mary had never met. They were like two hummingbirds who had also never met.'

❋

'Shots rang out, as shots are wont to do.'

❋

'She walked into my office like a centipede with ninety-eight missing legs.'

❋

'It hurt the way your tongue hurts after you accidentally staple it to the wall.'

GENUINE THINGS WRITTEN BY SCHOOL STUDENTS IN HISTORY ESSAYS

'In midevil times most people were alliterate.'

❋

'The Bible is full of interesting caricatures. In the first book of the Bible, Guinessis, Adam and Eve were created from an apple tree. One of their children, Cain, asked, "Am I my brother's son?"'

❋

'Queen Elizabeth was the "Virgin Queen". As a queen she was a success. When she exposed herself before her troops they all shouted "hurrah".'

132

'Socrates was a famous Greek teacher who went around giving people advice. They killed him. Socrates died from an overdose of wedlock. After his death, his career suffered a dramatic decline.'

✳

'Moses led the Hebrew slaves to the Red Sea, where they made unleavened bread which is bread made without any ingredients. Moses went up on Mount Cyanide to get the ten commandments. He died before he ever reached Canada.'

✳

'Finally Magna Carta provided that no man should be hanged twice for the same offense.'

✳

'Another story was William Tell, who shot an arrow through an apple while standing on his son's head.'

✳

'Eventually, the Romans conquered the Greeks. History calls people Romans because they never stayed in one place for very long.'

'The First World War, caused by the assignation of the Arch-Duck by an anahist, ushered in a new error in the anals of human history.'

'Beethoven wrote music even though he was deaf. He was so deaf he wrote loud music.'

'The sun never set on the British Empire because the British Empire is in the East and the sun sets in the West. Queen Victoria was the longest queen. She sat on a thorn for 63 years. She was a moral woman who practised virtue. Her death was the final event which ended her reign.'

'The nineteenth century was a time of a great many thoughts and inventions. People stopped reproducing by hand and started reproducing by machine. The invention of the steamboat caused a network of rivers to spring up. Cyrus McCormick invented the McCormick raper, which did the work of a hundred men. Louis Pasteur discovered a cure for rabbis. Charles Darwin was a naturalist who wrote the Organ of the Species. Madman Curie discovered radio. And Karl Marx became one of the Marx brothers.'

'The Greeks were a highly sculptured people, and without them we wouldn't have history.'

WHERE'S IT FROM?

CABINET

A Prime Minister's cabinet goes back to the days before Prime Ministers when the king (or queen) governed the country. Kings too needed advisers and they used to meet with them in small private rooms called 'cabinets' to discuss matters of state. From this word, we get the modern cabinet.

GENUINE ANSWERS GIVEN BY SCHOOL
STUDENTS IN SCIENCE TESTS

'The body consists of three parts: the brainium, the borax
and the abominable cavity. The brainium contains the
brain, the borax contains the heart and lungs, and the
abominable cavity contains the bowls, of which there are
five – a, e, i, o and u.'

✳

'When you breathe, you inspire.
When you do not breathe, you expire.'

✳

'When you smell an odourless gas, it is probably
carbon monoxide.'

✳

'Three kinds of blood vessels are arteries,
vanes and caterpillars.'

✳

'Nitrogen is not found in Ireland because it is not
found in a free state.'

✳

'H_2O is hot water, and CO_2 is cold water.'

✳

'Blood flows down one leg and up the other.'

✳

'To keep milk from turning sour, keep it in the cow.'

135

'Water is composed of two gins, Oxygin and Hydrogin. Oxygin is pure gin. Hydrogin is gin and water.'

✳

'A fossil is an extinct animal. The older it is, the more extinct it is.'

'Dew is formed on leaves when the sun shines down on them and makes them perspire.'

'Artifical insemination is when the farmer does it to the cow instead of the bull.'

✳

'The tides are a fight between the earth and moon. All water tends towards the moon, because there is no water in the moon, and nature abhors a vacuum. I forget where the sun joins in this fight.'

✳

'Germinate: To become a naturalized German.'

✳

'Momentum: What you give a person when they are going away.'

GENUINE COMMENTS MADE BY AMERICAN TEACHERS ON STUDENTS' REPORT CARDS*

'Your son sets low personal standards and then consistently fails to achieve them.'

✳

'Your son is depriving a village somewhere of an idiot.'

✳

'Your child has delusions of adequacy.'

✳

'Since my last report, your child has reached rock bottom and has started to dig.'

✳

'I would not allow this student to breed.'

✳

'The student has a "full six-pack" but lacks the plastic thing to hold it all together.'

✳

'This child has been working with glue too much.'

✳

'The gates are down, the lights are flashing, but the train isn't coming.'

✳

'If this student were any more stupid, he'd have to be watered twice a week.'

'It's impossible to believe the sperm that created this child beat out 1,000,000 others.'

✳

'The wheel is turning but the hamster is definitely dead.'

*All teachers were reprimanded

WHERE'S IT FROM?

SIDEKICK

In America's Wild West of the late nineteenth century, friends you rode with were known as side-pals and side-partners – because they rode at your side. Sometimes, they were also called side-kickers because, in the language of the time, you kicked along together. This got shortened to side-kicks and, over time, the hyphen was lost and it became 'sidekicks'.

Genuine Things Written to Tax and Welfare Authorities

'I am glad to report that my husband who was reported missing is dead.'

❖

'It is true I am a bachelor and have deducted for two children. But please believe me when I say it was an accident.'

❖

'You have changed my little boy to a little girl. Will this make any difference?'

❖

'I cannot pay the full amount at the moment as my husband is in hospital. As soon as I can I will send on the remains.'

❖

'If my husband puts in a claim for a dependent named Marcia, I just want you to know that my name is Gertrude.'

❖

'Do I have to pay taxes on the alimony my former husband is paying me? It's not as though I do anything to earn it.'

'I have to inform you that my mother-in-law passed away after receiving your form on 22 November. Thanking you.'

◆

'Please send me a claim form as I have had a baby. I had one before, but it got dirty and I burned it.'

◆

'Please correct this assessment. I have not worked for the past three months as I have broken my leg. Hoping you will do the same.'

◆

'Re your request for a P45 for a new employee. You already have it and he isn't leaving here but coming, so we haven't got it.'

◆

'I have not been living with my husband for several years, and have much pleasure in enclosing his last will and testament.'

◆

'I cannot get sick pay. I have six children, can you tell me why?'

◆

'I want money as quick as I can get it. I have been in bed with the doctor for two weeks and this doesn't seem to do me any good. If things don't improve I will be forced to send for another doctor.'

'I am writing to the Welfare Department to say that my baby was born two years old. When do I get my money?'

'Unless I get my money soon, I will be forced to lead an immortal life.'

'In accordance with your instructions, I have given birth to twins in the enclosed envelope.'

'Mrs Jones has not had any clothes for a year and has been visited regularly by the clergy.'

'I am very annoyed that you have branded my son illiterate, as this is a lie. I was married to his father a week before he was born.'

'Please send me an official letter advising that I can't claim the costs of taking my wife to conventions. I don't want her along but I need an excuse.'

'Thank you for explaining my income tax liability. You have done it so clearly that I almost understand it.'

Genuine Responses Given by Mothers to the Child Support Office

'Regarding the identity of the father of my twins, child A was fathered by [name given]. I am unsure as to the identity of the father of child B, but I believe that he was conceived on the same night.'

'From the dates it seems that my daughter was conceived at EuroDisney. Maybe it really is the Magic Kingdom.'

'I do not know the name of the father of my little girl. She was conceived at a party at [address given] where I had unprotected sex with a man I met that night. I do remember that the sex was so good that I fainted. If you do manage to track down the father can you send me his phone number? Thanks.'

★

'I don't know the identity of the father of my daughter. He drives a BMW that now has a hole made by my stiletto in one of the door panels. Perhaps you can contact BMW service stations in this area and see if he's had it replaced?'

'I have never had sex with a man. I am awaiting a letter from the Pope confirming that my son's conception was immaculate and that he is Christ risen again.'

★

'I cannot tell you the name of child A's dad as he informs me that to do so would blow his cover and that would have cataclysmic implications for the economy. I am torn between doing right by you and right by the country. Please advise.'

★

'[name given] is the father of child A. If you do catch up with him can you ask him what he did with my AC/DC CDs.'

★

'I am unsure as to the identity of the father of my baby. After all, when you eat a can of beans you can't be sure which one made you fart.'

WHERE'S IT FROM?

WHY AMERICANS CALL THE AUTUMN 'FALL'

From the late seventeenth century, fall was the word for the third season of the year used by people on both sides of the Atlantic. It wasn't until the eighteenth century that the Brits began to use the fourteenth-century word 'autumn' which was derived from the French while the Americans continued to use fall.

Genuine Announcements Made by Airline Staff

'Welcome aboard Southwest Flight 245 to Tampa. To operate your seat belt, insert the metal tab into the buckle, and pull tight. It works just like every other seat belt; and if you don't know how to operate one, you probably shouldn't be out in public unsupervised.'

'People, people, we're not picking out furniture here, find a seat and get in it!'

'We'd like to thank you folks for flying with us today. And, the next time you get the insane urge to go blasting through the skies in a pressurized metal tube, we hope you'll think of US Airways.'

'Ladies and gentlemen, we've reached cruising altitude and will be turning down the cabin lights. This is for your comfort and to enhance the appearance of your flight attendants.'

'There may be fifty ways to leave your lover, but there are only four ways out of this airplane.'

'Thank you for flying Delta Business Express.
We hope you enjoyed giving us the business as much as we
enjoyed taking you for a ride.'

'In the event of a sudden loss of cabin pressure,
masks will descend from the ceiling. Stop screaming, grab
the mask, and pull it over your face. If you have a small
child travelling with you, secure your mask before
assisting with theirs. If you are travelling with more than
one small child, pick your favourite.'

'Weather at our destination is fifty degrees with some
broken clouds, but we'll try to have them fixed before
we arrive. Thank you, and remember, nobody loves you,
or your money, more than Southwest Airlines.'

'Your seat cushions can be used for flotation, and, in
the event of an emergency water landing, please paddle to
shore and take them with our compliments.'

'As you exit the plane, make sure to gather all of your
belongings. Anything left behind will be distributed
evenly among the flight attendants. Please do not leave
children or spouses.'

'Delta Airlines is pleased to have some of the best flight attendants in the industry. Unfortunately, none of them are on this flight!'

'Ladies and gentlemen, if you wish to smoke, the smoking section on this airplane is on the wing and if you can light 'em, you can smoke 'em.'

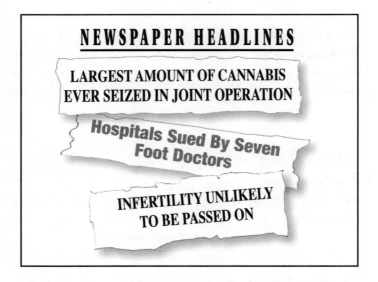

NEWSPAPER HEADLINES

LARGEST AMOUNT OF CANNABIS
EVER SEIZED IN JOINT OPERATION

Hospitals Sued By Seven
Foot Doctors

INFERTILITY UNLIKELY
TO BE PASSED ON

A Word to the Wise 4

Did you know...

The name **jeep** came from the abbreviation **GP**, used in the army for general-purpose vehicle.

✦

There are only two words in the English language ending in **-gry**: **hungry** and **angry.**

✦

The word **had** can be used eleven times in a row in the following sentence about two boys, John and Steve, who had written similar sentences in their essays: *John, where Steve had had 'had', had had 'had had'; 'had had' had had the higher mark.*

✦

The word **and** can be used five times in a row in the following sentence about a sign being painted above a shop called Jones And Son: *Mr Jones looks at the sign and says to the painter, 'I would like bigger gaps between Jones and and, and and and Son.'*

✦

The words **loosen** and **unloosen** mean the same thing.

✦

The first letters of the months July to November spell the name **JASON**.

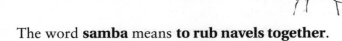

Hippopotomonstrosesquippedaliophobia
is the fear of long words.

The word **samba** means **to rub navels together**.

◆

Cerumen is the technical term for **earwax**.

◆

The oldest word in the English language is **town**.

◆

The word **coffee** came from Arabic and meant **excitement**.

◆

The word **voodoo** comes from a West African word that means **spirit** or **deity** and has no negative connotations.

◆

The phrase **sleep tight** originated when ropes round a wooden frame were used to support a mattress. Sagging ropes could be tightened with a bed key.

◆

The youngest letters in the English language are **j**, **v** and **w**.

◆

The names for the numbers **eleven** and **twelve** in English come from the Anglo-Saxon for **one left** (*aend-lefene*) and **two left** (*twa-lefene*). They represented going back to your left hand and starting again after reaching ten counting on your fingers.

The stars and colours you see when you rub your eyes are
called **phosphenes**.

✦

No word in the English language rhymes with **pint**,
diamond or **purple**.

The magic word **abracadabra** was
originally intended for the specific
purpose of curing hay fever.

WHERE'S IT FROM?

THE USE OF THE WORD 'GAY'
TO MEAN HOMOSEXUAL

The word 'gay' has had a long history. In 1637, the
Oxford English Dictionary gave one meaning for gay
as 'addicted to social pleasures and dissipations; of
loose and immoral life'. By the nineteenth century, the
word was associated with prostitutes. There wasn't any
homosexual usage of the word until the twentieth century
when there are several different possibilities, including the
word 'geycat' to describe a homosexual boy and that gay,
in the sense of 'cheerful and bright', was probably used to
describe effeminate men and it stuck. It's not true that the
usage came from the acronym 'Good As You' – as seen on
placards in gay rights marches of the 1970s: the acronym
comes from the word gay and not the other way round.

Genuine Car Bumper Stickers

CAUTION: I drive just like you!

Don't Drink and Drive – you might spill some

**This car is insured by the Mafia – you hit me,
they hit you**

Be careful – 90 per cent of people are caused by accidents

Sorry, I don't date outside my species

Rehab is for Quitters

Not all dumbs are blonde

I took an IQ test and the results were negative

I don't brake for pedestrians

If you lived in your car, you'd be home by now

WHERE'S IT FROM?

DUNCE'S CAP

In days gone by, children who underachieved at school would be put in the corner and made to wear a conical-shaped dunce's cap. The first person to wear the dunce's cap was the man after whom it was actually named: John Duns Scotus, an Oxford theologian of the fourteenth century who thought the conical hat would help him receive messages from God.

Fast forward a couple of centuries and philosophers were sneering at John Duns Scotus and his followers – known as Dunses or, later, Dunces. And so the conical-shaped dunce's cap became associated with stupidity.

Honk if you've been married to Elizabeth Taylor

If you think I'm a lousy driver, you should see me putt

Learn from your parents' mistakes – use birth control

Of course I'm drunk – what do you think I am,
a stunt driver?

Eat Well, Stay Fit, Die Anyway

YOU! Out of the gene pool!

151

You can't drink all day long if you don't start first thing in the morning

If you don't like the way I drive, get off the pavement

How many roads must a man travel down before he admits he is lost?

I'm not a complete idiot – some parts are missing

He who laughs last thinks slowest

Instant asshole, just add alcohol

Beer isn't just for breakfast

NEWSPAPER HEADLINES

New Study of Obesity Looks for Larger Test Group

Stiff opposition expected to casketless funeral plan

Mad Cow Talks

Proverbs That Are Clearly Not True

An apple a day keeps the doctor away.

✳

You can't judge a book by its cover.

✳

You can't have your cake and eat it.

✳

The best things in life are free.

✳

Every cloud has a silver lining.

✳

Ask no questions and you will be told no lies.

✳

Barking dogs seldom bite.

✳

There is no accounting for taste.

✳

The race is not to the swift.

✳

It never rains but it pours.

Wonderfully Titled Books

A Century of Sand Dredging in the Bristol Channel:
Volume Two

A Taxonomy of Office Chairs

Afterthoughts of a Worm Hunter

Collectible Spoons of the Third Reich

Natural Bust Enlargement with Total Power:
How to Increase the Other 90% of Your Mind
to Increase the Size of Your Breasts

The Great Singapore Penis Panic: And the
Future of American Mass Hysteria

Cooking with Poo (NB: 'Poo' is Thai for 'crab')

Crocheting Adventures with Hyperbolic Planes

Egg Banjos from Around the World

Estonian Sock Patterns All Around the World

Governing Lethal Behavior in Autonomous Robots

Greek Rural Postmen and Their Cancellation Numbers

Highlights in the History of Concrete

How to Avoid Huge Ships

How to Conduct a One-Day Conference on Death Education

I Stopped Sucking My Thumb . . . Why Can't You Stop Drinking?

Japanese Chins

Lesbian Sadomasochism Safety Manual

Reusing Old Graves

Development in Dairy Cow Breeding and Management and New Opportunities to Widen the Uses of Straw

Weeds in a Changing World

High Performance Stiffened Structures

The Big Book of Lesbian Horse Stories

Living with Crazy Buttocks

Managing a Dental Practice the Genghis Khan Way

Mr Andoh's Pennine Diary: Memoirs of a Japanese Chicken Sexer in 1935 Hebden Bridge

People Who Don't Know They're Dead: How They Attach Themselves to Unsuspecting Bystanders and What to Do About It

Proceedings of the Second International Workshop on Nude Mice

The 2009–2014 World Outlook for 60-milligram Containers of Fromage Frais

The Book of Marmalade: Its Antecedents, Its History, and Its Role in the World Today

The Large Sieve and its Applications

The Mushroom in Christian Art

The Stray Shopping Carts of Eastern North America: A Guide to Field Identification

What do Socks do?

What Kind of Bean is This Chihuahua?

WHERE'S IT FROM?

SHERIFF

This is derived from 'Shire Reeve'. During early years of feudal rule in England, each shire had a reeve who was the law for that shire. When the term was brought to the United States it was shortened to Sheriff.

The First Lines of Classic Novels

'It was a bright cold day in April, and the
clocks were striking thirteen.'
1984 BY GEORGE ORWELL

★

'Hale knew, before he had been in Brighton three
hours, that they meant to murder him.'
BRIGHTON ROCK BY GRAHAM GREENE

★

'As Gregor Samsa woke one morning from uneasy
dreams he found himself transformed in his bed
into a gigantic insect.'
METAMORPHOSIS BY FRANZ KAFKA

★

'Last night I dreamed I went to Manderley again.'
REBECCA BY DAPHNE DU MAURIER

★

'Happy families are all alike, but an unhappy family
is unhappy in its own way.'
ANNA KARENINA BY LEO TOLSTOY

★

'There were 117 psychoanalysts on the Pan Am flight to
Vienna and I'd been treated by at least six of them.'
FEAR OF FLYING BY ERICA JONG

'What's it going to be then, eh?'
A CLOCKWORK ORANGE BY ANTHONY BURGESS

★

'Many years later, as he faced the firing squad,
Colonel Aureliano Buendía was to remember that distant
afternoon when his father took him to discover ice.'
ONE HUNDRED YEARS OF SOLITUDE
BY GABRIEL GARCÍA MÁRQUEZ

★

'Stately, plump Buck Mulligan came from the
stairhead, bearing a bowl of lather on which a mirror
and a razor lay crossed.'
ULYSSES BY JAMES JOYCE

★

'I'm going to get that bloody bastard if
I die in the attempt.'
KING RAT BY JAMES CLAVELL

★

'On top of everything, the cancer wing was number 13.'
CANCER WARD BY ALEXANDER SOLZHENITSYN

★

'If you really want to hear about it, the first thing
you'll probably want to know is where I was born, and
what my lousy childhood was like and how my parents
were occupied and all before they had me, and all that
David Copperfield kind of crap, but I don't feel like going
into it, if you want to know the truth.'
THE CATCHER IN THE RYE BY J.D. SALINGER

Genuine Song Titles

'I'd Rather Be A Lobster Than A Wiseguy'
EDWARD MADDEN AND THEODORE F. MORSE, 1907

✦

('Potatoes Are Cheaper – Tomatoes Are Cheaper)
Now's The Time To Fall In Love'
AL LEWIS AND AL SHERMAN, 1931

✦

'Hey Young Fella Close Your Old Umbrella'
DOROTHY FIELDS AND JIMMY MCHUGH, 1933

✦

'Who Ate Napoleons With Josephine
When Bonaparte Was Away'
WRITTEN BY ALFRED BRYAN AND E. RAY GOTZ IN 1920

✦

'Aunt Jemima And Your Uncle Cream of Wheat'
JOHNNY MERCER AND RUBE BLOOM, 1936

✦

'Come After Breakfast, Bring 'Long Your Lunch And
Leave 'Fore Supper Time'
J. TIM BRYMAN, CHRIS SMITH AND JAMES HENRY BURRIS, 1909

✦

'I Love To Dunk A Hunk of Sponge Cake'
CLARENCE GASKILL, 1928

'Caldonia (What Makes Your Big Head So Hard)'
FLEECIE MOORE, 1946

'All The Quakers Are Shoulder Shakers Down
In Quaker Town'
BERT KALMAR, EDGAR LESLIE AND PETE WENDLING, 1919

GREAT COUNTRY AND WESTERN TITLES

'Everything You Touch Turns to Dirt'

'Get Your Tongue Outta My Mouth 'Cause I'm
Kissing You Goodbye'

'Heaven's Just A Sin Away'

'Her Teeth Were Stained, But Her Heart Was Pure'

'How Can I Miss You If You Won't Go Away?'

'I've Been A Liar All My Life'

'I Changed Her Oil, She Changed My Life

'I Don't Know Whether To Kill Myself Or Go Bowling'

'I Forgot More Than You'll Ever Know'

◆

'I Gave Her A Ring, She Gave Me The Finger'

◆

'I Keep Forgettin' I Forgot About You'

◆

'I Liked You Better Before I Knew You So Well'

◆

'I Married Her Just Because She Looks Like You'

◆

'I Wouldn't Take Her To A Dawg Fight, 'Cause
I'm Afraid She'd Win'

◆

'I'll Marry You Tomorrow But Let's Honeymoon Tonite'

◆

'I'm Gonna Hire A Wino To Decorate Our Home'

◆

'I've Got You On My Conscience But At Least
You're Off My Back'

◆

'If Drinkin' Don't Kill Me Her Memory Will'

◆

'If Whiskey Were A Woman I'd Be Married For Sure'

'If You Don't Believe I Love You Just Ask My Wife'

◆

'If You Leave Me, Can I Come Too?'

◆

'My Wife Ran Off With My Best Friend,
And I Sure Do Miss Him'

◆

'She Got The Goldmine (I Got the Shaft)'

◆

'She Used My Tears to Wash Her Socks'

◆

'She's Actin' Single (I'm Drinkin' Doubles)'

◆

'The Last Word In Lonesome Is "Me"'

◆

'The Next Time You Throw That Fryin' Pan,
My Face Ain't Gonna Be There'

◆

'When You Leave Walk Out Backwards,
So I'll Think You're Walking In'

◆

'You Just Hurt My Last Feeling'

◆

'You're The Reason Our Kids Are Ugly'

Words Around the World

The Hawaiian alphabet has only twelve letters.

Jenga means 'to build' in Swahili.

In Korean, there are no words for 'brother' or 'sister',
but there are words for an older or younger brother,
and an older or younger sister.

In Chinese, the words 'crisis' and 'opportunity'
are the same.

There is no Albanian
word for headache.

TAXI is spelled the same way in English, French,
German, Swedish, Spanish, Danish, Norwegian, Dutch,
Czech and Portuguese.

The word 'mafia' was created as an acronym for
Morte alla francia italia adela, meaning 'Death to the
French is Italy's cry'.

The Albanian language, one of Europe's oldest, is not derived from any other language. And the alphabet was invented as recently as 1908. It contains thirty-six letters but no 'w'.

The German language combines words to make composite words. So, for example, the single German word for 'Favourite break-time sandwich' is *Lieblingspausenbrot*.

The Lao language has no words ending in 's'. So they call their country Lao instead of Laos.

There's a Mexican language named Zoque-Ayapeneco which has withered away until there were just two people in the whole world who spoke it. The   trouble is that those two men – both in their seventies – hate each other and refuse to speak to one another.

The Lozi language of Zambia has at least forty words meaning 'woman'. Each describes a woman at a particular stage in life. For example, an unmarried woman, a newlywed just arrived in her husband's village, a widow etc.

In the Malay language, plurals are formed by repeating the word. For example, the Malay word for 'man' is *laki* so the word for 'men' is *laki-laki*.

Romanian words sound similar to some Italian, French or Spanish words because Romania is the only country in Eastern Europe where people speak a language of Latin origin.

There are African languages that have fewer than a hundred people speaking (each of) them. The reason a language has so few speakers is because those people who speak it live in a closed community cut off from most of the rest of the world. As the world discovers them and they discover the world, they're obliged to learn a more popular language and so their native language dies.

Nearly half of all Germans are fluent in English, but only three per cent of Germans speak French fluently.

In Bulgaria, shaking the head from side to side means yes and nodding up and down means no.

Because of the mix of cultures and languages, many Mauritians are multilingual. A person might speak

Bhojpuri at home, French to a supervisor at work, English to a government official and Creole to friends.

Many people in the Syrian town of Ma'loula still speak Aramaic, the language spoken by Jesus of Nazareth.

English teenagers learn the fewest languages in Europe.
On average, they learn 0.6 of a language
(it sounds preposterous but it *is* an average!)
as opposed to the 1.4 languages that the average
teenager learns in other EU countries.

A lot of modern English first names come from
Greek words.

NEWSPAPER HEADLINES

**LAWYERS GIVE POOR
FREE LEGAL ADVICE**

**MISSIPPI'S LITERACY PROGRAM
SHOWS IMPROVEMENT**

**Police begin campaign
to run down jaywalkers**

The molars that grow between the ages of seventeen and twenty-five are known as wisdom teeth in the UK but in Romania they're known as 'mind teeth' and in Korea they're called 'love teeth'.

The phrase 'running amok' is derived from the Papua New Guinean word *amok* meaning 'rage'.

The word Blighty comes from *bilayti*, the Urdu for 'homeland'.

English has borrowed many words from Arabic. A few are: alkali, caraway, checks, chemistry, saffron and satin.

In South Africa the @ symbol is referred to as an *aapstert* which means a 'monkey's tail'. In Israel, it's called a *strudel*, in Slovakia, it's known as a 'pickled herring' while in Denmark it's often called an 'elephant's trunk'.

The word 'thug' comes from the Hindu word *thag* which referred to the religious fanatics who plagued India, carrying out acts of brutality in the name of their goddess.

In Guyana, the same phrases and sentences are used for both questions and statements. You can tell the difference by the way the words are spoken – by their tone. So, for example, the statement: 'Ben is doing well at school', spoken in a flat, even tone, means that Ben is doing well at school. The same words said in a higher pitch and a questioning tone means 'Is Ben doing well at school?'

Polish has some lovely names for months. For example, April in Polish means 'flowers', July means 'linden tree', September means 'heather' and November translates as 'falling leaves'.

The Manx language is taught in almost every school on the Isle of Man.

Between the seventeenth and nineteenth centuries, French was the language of diplomacy and culture in Europe, and many northern European monarchs spoke it in their courts. Today, there are some 125 million French speakers worldwide.

Jamaicans refer to their major crops in terms of gold. Sugar is brown gold, bananas are green gold, bauxite is red gold and citrus fruits are sun gold.

Sanskrit is considered as the mother of all higher languages.

Over 800 different languages are spoken in Papua New Guinea. With a population of just over six million people, that's about one language for every 7,500 people. The result of this is that there are villages within five miles of each other which speak different languages.

Asia has the most languages and the most speakers, accounting for sixty-one per cent of all language speakers in the world.

Africa has the second largest number of languages after Asia but accounts for under twelve per cent of all the world's language speakers.

In the Netherlands, they have a wonderful expression of amazement that translates as 'That breaks my clog'. The sturdy wooden clog is still worn by some Dutch farmers because it is waterproof in damp fields.

Luxembourg has its own language – Luxembourgish – which is also sometimes spoken in parts of Belgium, France and Germany.

The Filipino language reflects the importance of rice to the Filipino people. Their language has several words for rice, including words to mean rice that is harvested but not cleaned, rice that is still cooking in a pot and rice that is ready to eat.

Irish words that have entered the English language include banshee, galore, bother, smithereen, hooligan, tantrum and donnybrook.

The Phoenician alphabet, which was in use around 1600 BC, is widely considered the foundation for alphabetic writing in the West and Middle East.

NEWSPAPER HEADLINES

Complaints about referees growing ugly

BULGE IN TROUSERS WAS ECSTASY

Golfers warned not to lick balls

COUNTRIES THAT HAVE **ENGLISH** AS THEIR OFFICIAL LANGUAGE (OR ONE OF THEM)

American Samoa, Anguilla,
Antigua and Barbuda,
Ascension Islands, Australia,
The Bahamas, Barbados,
Belize, Bermuda, Botswana
Cameroon, Canada,
Cayman Islands,
Channel Islands,
Christmas Island,
Cook Islands
Dominica, Dutch Antilles
Falkland Islands, Fiji
The Gambia, Ghana,
Gibraltar, Grenada, Guam,
Guyana
Hong Kong
Ireland, Isle of Man
Jamaica
Kiribati
Liberia
Madagascar, Malawi

Marshall Islands, Mauritius,
Montserrat
Namibia, Nauru,
New Zealand, Nigeria,
Palau, Papua New Guinea,
Pitcairn Islands, Puerto Rico
St Kitts & Nevis, St Lucia,
Samoa, Seychelles,
Sierra Leone, Singapore,
Solomon Islands,
South Africa, Sudan,
Swaziland
Tonga,
Trinidad and Tobago,
Tristan da Cunha,
Turks and Caicos Islands,
Tuvalu
Uganda, United Kingdom,
United States of America
Vanuatu
Zambia, Zimbabwe

COUNTRIES THAT HAVE **FRENCH** AS THEIR OFFICIAL LANGUAGE (OR ONE OF THEM)

Algeria
Belgium, Benin,
Burkina Faso, Burundi
Cameroon, Canada,
Central African Republic,
Chad, Comoros, Congo
Democratic Republic of
Congo, Djibouti
Equatorial Guinea
France, French Guiana,
French Polynesia
Gabon, Guadeloupe, Guinea

Haiti
Ivory Coast
Luxembourg
Madagascar, Mali,
Martinique, Mauritania,
Monaco
New Caledonia, Niger
Reunion Senegal,
The Seychelles, Switzerland
Togo
Vanuatu
Wallis and Futuna

COUNTRIES THAT HAVE **SPANISH** AS THEIR OFFICIAL LANGUAGE (OR ONE OF THEM)

Argentina
Bolivia
Chile, Colombia,
Costa Rica, Cuba
Dominican Republic
Ecuador, El Salvador,
Equatorial Guinea
Guatemala

Honduras
Mexico
Nicaragua
Panama, Paraguay, Peru,
Puerto Rico
Spain, Uruguay
Venezuela

COUNTRIES THAT HAVE **PORTUGUESE** AS THEIR OFFICIAL LANGUAGE (OR ONE OF THEM)

Angola	Guinea-Bissau
Brazil	Mozambique
Cape Verde	Portugal
East Timor	Sao Tome and Principe
Equatorial Guinea	Uruguay

COUNTRIES THAT HAVE **GERMAN** AS THEIR OFFICIAL LANGUAGE (OR ONE OF THEM)

Austria	Liechtenstein
Belgium	Luxembourg
Germany	Switzerland

COUNTRIES THAT HAVE **DUTCH** AS THEIR OFFICIAL LANGUAGE (OR ONE OF THEM)

Aruba	Netherlands
Belgium	Suriname
Dutch Antilles	

COUNTRIES THAT HAVE **ITALIAN** AS THEIR OFFICIAL LANGUAGE (OR ONE OF THEM)

Italy	Switzerland
San Marino	Vatican City

A Guide to Strine
(Australian Slang)

The way that Australians speak is known as 'Strine'. This word is thought to be the word 'Australian' spoken through closed teeth. Some scholars say this pronunciation came about because of the need to keep one's mouth shut against blow flies.

The novelist Monica Dickens might have had a part in identifying the phenomenon. The story goes that in 1964 she was on a book tour of Australia when she was approached by a woman who handed her a copy of her book and asked 'How much is it?' Because of the woman's accent, the author thought she'd asked her to autograph the book to 'Emma Chisit' and duly signed the book. This led to much hilarity and correspondence in Australian newspapers and 'Strine' was duly identified and entered the lexicon.

To bend the elbow – to have a drink

Bonza or *beaut* – wonderful, great

Chook – chicken

Crook – unwell

Dead as a dead dingo's donga – in a parlous condition

To drink with the flies – to drink alone

Dunny – toilet

Fair dinkum – the real thing

Fair go – good chance

Godzone – God's own country (i.e. Australia)

Grog – booze ('BYOG' on an invitation means bring your own grog)

Hit your kick – open your wallet

Hooly dooly – I say

Ripper – super

A sausage short of a barbie – not in possession of all (his) faculties

She'll be right – no problem

Spunky – good-looking

True blue – honest or straight

Tucker – food

Wowser – killjoy, spoilsport

NEWSPAPER HEADLINES

THREAT DISRUPTS PLANS TO MEET ABOUT THREATS

HOME SECRETARY TO ACT ON VIDEO NASTIES

Dead Man Remains Dead

How to Say 'Beer' in Different Languages

cerveza (Spanish)
cerveja (Portuguese)
sor (Hungarian)
bière (French)
Bier (German)
bjór (Icelandic)
pombe (Swahili)
pivo (Russian)
öl (Swedish)

øl (Danish and Norwegian)
olut (Finnish)
bira (Turkish)
bir (Indonesian)
bere (Romanian)
birra (Italian)
beera (Greek)
fermentum/cervisia (Latin)

WHERE'S IT FROM?

TOADY

This derives its meaning as a sycophant from the word the 'toadeater' who was one half of an eighteenth-century pair of con artists. He would swallow a toad in public and then his partner would cure him with a 'magical elixir'.

Genuine Products From Abroad

Sor Bits (Danish mints)
Krapp (Scandinavian toilet paper)
Grand Dick (French red wine)
Nora Knackers (Norwegian biscuits)
Moron (Italian wine)
Mukki (Italian yoghurt)
Cock (French deodorant)
Plopp (Swedish toffee bar)
Bum (Turkish biscuits)
Donkee Basterd Suker (Dutch sugar)
Zit (Greek fizzy drink)
Bimbo Bread (South America)
Craps Chocolate (France)
Pschitt (French fizzy drink)
Grated Fanny (South American tinned fish)
Atum Bom (Portuguese tinned tuna)
Hot Piss (Japanese antifeeze spray)
I'm So Sorry Please Forgive Me (Swiss chocolate bar)
Bimbo (Mexican biscuits)
Vaccine (Dutch aftershave)
Flirt (Austrian cigarettes)
Meltykiss (Japanese chocolate)
Climax (Kenyan disinfectant)
Noisy (French butter)
Prison (Ugandan body spray)

Two Countries Separated by a Common Language

Americanisms And How They Translate Into English

acetaminophen (Tylenol) = paracetamol (Panadol)

arugula = rocket (herb)

bellhop = hotel porter

beltway = ring road

bleachers = stands (at sports grounds)

booger = bogey

boondocks = backwoods

boondoggle = scheme that wastes time and money

broil = grill (food)

bullhorn = megaphone

burglarize = burgle

busboy = assistant waiter

caboose = guard's van (on a train)

Canadian bacon = back bacon

comfort station = public toilet

crapshoot = risky venture

cremains = ashes

eggplant = aubergine

fanny pack = bum bag

faucet = tap
gasoline/gas = petrol
green thumb = green fingers (of a gardener)
grifter = con artist
grunt = soldier
half bath = (downstairs) washroom
hickey = love bite
play hooky = play truant
jackhammer = pneumatic drill
jelly = jam
Joe Public/Joe Schmoe = Joe Bloggs
kerosene = paraffin
mohawk = mohican (haircut)
mom-and-pop store = corner shop
mortician = undertaker
moxie = courage, daring
nightstick = truncheon
nix = cancel
ornery = irritable, cranky
pacifier = dummy
penny-ante = petty, insignificant
period = full stop
realtor = estate agent
RV park = caravan site
scallion = spring onion
scalper = ticket tout
sophomore = second-year college or high-school student

spelunking = caving or potholing
spyglass = telescope
station wagon = estate car
stickshift = a manual car
streetcar = tram
teeterboard = seesaw
zinger = witty, often caustic remark
zucchini = courgette

THINGS YOU CAN ORDER IN AN AMERICAN DINER – AND WHAT YOU'LL GET

Adam and Eve on a raft – two poached eggs on toast
Belch water – a glass of seltzer or soda water
Bowl of red – a serving of chili
Brown cow – chocolate milk
Cowboy with spurs – an omelette with chips
Eve with the lid on – apple pie
Murphy carrying a wreath – ham and potatoes with cabbage
Nervous pudding – jelly
Put out the lights and cry – liver with onions
Wreck a pair – two scrambled eggs

A Word to the Wise 5
Did you know...

John Milton used **8,000** different words in *Paradise Lost*.

The word **monosyllable** has five syllables.

Ten human body parts are only three letters
long: **eye, hip, arm, leg, ear, toe, jaw, rib, lip, gum**.

The suffix **-ology** means the study of something. The
shortest **-ology** is **oology – the study of eggs**.

The word **starboard** is derived from the Old English word
for the paddle that Vikings used on the right side of their
ships to steer: ***steorbord.***

There's no word for **weather** in the Hawaiian language –
presumably because the weather there is always so fine.

The average reader can read **275** words per minute.

The vocabulary of the average person consists of
5,000 to **6,000** words.

●

Subbookkeeper is the only word found in an English
dictionary with four pairs of double letters in a row.

●

St John's Wood is the only London Underground
station that doesn't contain any letters from
the word **mackerel**.

●

Forty is the only number that has its letters in
alphabetical order.

●

One is the only number with its letters in reverse
alphabetical order.

●

The nine words: **the, of, and, to, it, you, be, have** and
will make up a quarter of all the words used in English.

●

Polish is the only word in the English language that when
capitalized is changed from a noun or a verb
to a nationality.

●

Accommodate is the most misspelled word in English.

The Lord's Prayer contains just sixty-eight words.

●

If you take away a letter from the word **startling**, you'll form a new word every time: **startling, starting, staring, string, sting, sing, sin, in, I**

Buffalo Buffalo buffalo buffalo buffalo buffalo Buffalo buffalo is a grammatically correct sentence – given the following meanings of the word: the bison; a part of New York; to intimidate.

Fraternity used to be a term applied by groups of thieves to themselves.

●

Adding just one letter to the middle of the one-syllable world **smile** turns it into the three-syllable word **simile**.

●

The longest words with vertical symmetry (the left half is a mirror image of the right half) are **otto, maam**, and **toot.**

●

The word **infant** comes from the Latin words meaning **not speaking.**

The word **salary** is derived from the word **salt**. In Roman times, salt was often used instead of money.

No Hawaiian word ends in a consonant.

The words **polysyllabic, fifteen-lettered** and **unhyphenated** are all **autological** in that they truly describe themselves.

Couscous is the longest word in the English language such that you can't tell visually if it's been written in all upper case or all lower case letters.

The Old English word for **sneeze** is *fneosam*.

Strengthlessnesses, eighteen letters long, is the longest word in the English language with just one (repeated) vowel.

The word **lethologica** describes the state of forgetting the word you want.

Peanuts aren't nuts, they're legumes.

An **ant lion** is neither an ant nor a lion. It is the larval form of the lacewing fly.

Banana oil doesn't come from bananas, it's made from petroleum.

Camel-hair brushes are made from squirrel hair.

Leaves don't change colour in autumn. They look green because they contain chlorophyll. When the leaf dies, the chlorophyll disappears and the other colours, which were there all along, emerge.

Soda water doesn't contain soda.

The **actress Tuesday Weld** was born on a Friday.

There **wasn't a single pony** in the Pony Express, only horses.

There's **no cream** in Cream Crackers.

Venetian blinds were invented in Japan.

How Dogs Bark in Different Languages

Albanian: *ham ham*
Arabic: *haw haw, hab hab*
Bulgarian: *bow bow*
Cantonese: *wōu-wōu*
Catalan: *bup bup*
Czech: *haf haf*
Danish: *vuf vuf*
Dutch: *waf waf, woef woef*
English: *woof, bow wow*
Finnish: *hau hau, vuh vuh*
French: *ouah ouah, ouaf ouaf, wouf wouf*
German: *wau wau, waff waff, wuff wuff*
Greek: *ghav ghav, woof*
Hindi: *bho bho*
Hungarian: *vau vau*
Icelandic: *voff voff*
Indonesian: *guk guk*

Italian: *bau bau*
Japanese: *wan wan*
Korean: *meong meong*
Macedonian: *av av*
Mandarin: *wāng wāng*
Norwegian: *voff voff, vov vov*
Persian: *vaagh vaagh*
Polish: *hau hau*
Russian: *gav gav, tyaf tyaf*
Spanish: *guau guau*
Swedish: *vov vov, voff voff*
Tamil: *vovw-vovw, loll-loll, vazh vazh*
Vietnamese: *gâu gâu, sủa sủa*

NEWSPAPER HEADLINES

LEGISLATOR WANTS TOUGHER DEATH PENALTY

Low Pay Reason For Poverty, Study Says

WHY YOU WANT SEX CHANGES WITH AGE

People Who Gave Their Names to Things

Adolf 'Adi' Dassler – *Adidas*
Adolphe & Edouard-Jean Cointreau – *Cointreau*
Adolphe Sax – *Saxophone*
Alessandro Volta – *Volt*
Anders Celsius – *Celsius temperature scale*
André-Marie Ampère – *Ampere*
Anna Pavlova – *Pavlova*
Bartolomeo Eustachi – *Eustachian tube* (in the ear)
Charles Boycott – *Boycott*
Charles Ponzi – *Ponzi scheme* (a type of fraud)
Charles Richter – *Richter scale*
Colonel Jean Martinet – *Martinet*
Commodore Benedict – *Eggs Benedict*
Count Ferdinand von Zeppelin – *Zeppelin airship*

Count Stroganoff – *Beef Stroganoff*
Dame Nellie Melba – *Peach Melba* and *Melba toast*
Duke of Wellington – *Wellington boot*
Earl Silas Tupper – *Tupperware*
Edmund Clerihew Bentley – *Clerihew*

Etienne de Silhouette – *Silhouette*
Facundo Bacardí Massó – *Bacardi*
Francis Beaufort – *Beaufort scale*
Franz Mesmer – *Mesmerize*
Gabriel Fahrenheit – *Fahrenheit temperature scale*
General Ambrose Burnside – *Sideburns*
Georg Ohm – *Ohm*
George Ferris – *Ferris Wheel*
Giuseppe Garibaldi – *Garibaldi biscuit*
Gustave Eiffel – *Eiffel Tower*
Hans Geiger – *Geiger counter*
Heinrich Rudolf Hertz – *Hertz*
Henry S. Shrapnel – *Shrapnel*
James Prescott Joule – *Joule*
James Watt – *Watt*
Jean Nicot – *Nicotine*
Joel Roberts Poinsett – *Poinsettia*
John Macadam – *Macadamia nut*
John Montagu, 4th Earl of Sandwich – *Sandwich*
John Philip Sousa – *Sousaphone*
Joseph Pilates – *Pilates*
Joseph-Ignace Guillotin – *Guillotine* (even though he didn't invent it)
Jules Léotard – *Leotard*
Laszlo Bíro – *Biro*
Leonhart Fuchs – *Fuchsia*
Louis Antoine de Bougainville – *Bougainvillea*
Louis Braille – *Braille*
Louis de Béchamel – *Béchamel sauce*

Louis Pasteur – *Pasteurisation*
Luigi Galvani – *Galvanization*
Mikhail Kalashnikov – *Kalashnikov rifle*
Ned Ludd – *Luddite*
Oliver Winchester – *Winchester rifle*
Ray Dolby – *Dolby surround system*
Robert Bunsen – *Bunsen burner*
Robert Moog – *Moog synthesizer*
Roy Jacuzzi – *Jacuzzi bath*
Rudolf Diesel – *Diesel*
Samuel Colt – *Colt revolver*
Samuel Maverick – *Maverick*
Samuel Morse – *Morse code*

Sir George Everest – *Mount Everest*
Sir Henry Bessemer – *Bessemer process* (for steel production)
Sir Isaac Newton – *Newton*
Sir William Gage – *Greengage*
Uziel Gal – *Uzi submachine gun*
William Fox – *20th Century Fox*
William Harley and Arthur Davidson – *Harley-Davidson*

ALL THE CHEMICAL ELEMENTS
NAMED AFTER PEOPLE

Curium: Marie Curie
Einsteinium: Albert Einstein
Fermium: Italian nuclear physicist Enrico Fermi
Gadolinium: Finnish chemist Johann Gadolin
Hahnium: German chemist Otto Hahn
Lawrencium: American physicist Ernest Lawrence
Mendelevium: Siberian chemist Dmitri Mendeleev
Rutherfordium: New Zealand physicist Ernest Rutherford

NEWSPAPER HEADLINES

STATISTICS SHOW THAT TEEN
PREGNANCY DROPS OFF
SIGNIFICANTLY AFTER AGE 25

HOMICIDE VICTIMS
RARELY TALK TO POLICE

March Planned
For Next August